Anonymous

Slavery, or Involuntary Servitude

Does it legally exist in the state of New York? Points on argument in Court

of appeals.

Anonymous

Slavery, or Involuntary Servitude
Does it legally exist in the state of New York? Points on argument in Court of appeals.

ISBN/EAN: 9783337403171

Printed in Europe, USA, Canada, Australia, Japan

Cover: Foto ©Suzi / pixelio.de

More available books at **www.hansebooks.com**

SLAVERY,

OR

INVOLUNTARY SERVITUDE:

DOES IT LEGALLY EXIST

IN THE

STATE OF NEW YORK?

POINTS ON ARGUMENT IN COURT OF APPEALS.

OPINIONS IN COURT OF APPEALS.

ALBANY:
J. MUNSELL, 78 STATE STREET.
1864.

SLAVERY, OR INVOLUNTARY SERVITUDE.

To Martinus Lansing, William Heidorn, William Witbeck, David
   Rector, John N. Smith, Albert Slingerland, John Ried, Nicholas
   Houck, Lawrence Fenner, Peter Ball, Denison Fish, Thomas B.
   Petrie, Jacob White, Louis Allendorph, John D. Wood, DeWitt
   C. Thomas, William Carmichael, and others.

GENTLEMEN ;

Having been employed by you to resist demands of rent made by
parties who have falsely assumed to be your landlords, we take this
mode of addressing you upon that subject. We trust we have an excuse,
if an excuse be necessary, in the importance of the questions involved,
and the fact that so great a number are directly interested, and re-
side so remote from each other, that it would be exceedingly incon-
venient, if not impracticable, to communicate personally, or address
you individually.

The immediate occasion for allowing you opportunity of informa-
tion, arises from the latest decisions of the Courts. Copies of the opinions are annexed. · But to read them understandingly, you should take
a brief retrospect of the past. To aid you in that respect, we will direct your attention to some of the more prominent aspects which the
subject has been made to assume, and the remarkable mutations which
have attended its progress.

The practical question forced upon you, was, whether you were *persons held to service* according to the laws of this State, and liable to forfeiture of your property for refusing to serve.

So far the question is personal to yourselves, and comparatively
unimportant to the public. But as there are no facts or circumstan-
ces pressing upon you, except such as are common to great numbers
of men, and capable of extension so as to embrace every owner of land
in the state, there are great public questions involved, namely; whether we have, in this State, an institution of servitude ; and, if so,
whether it is a relic of the past soon to wear out, or a thing just be-
gining life and vigor, fitted to grow and expand to an indefinite extent ; whether it came from the feudal contrivances used for the op-
pression of labor in the Old World or is one of our own : and, if
the latter, by what malign influences it was generated and nourish-
ed, and is now sustained in the midst of our free institutions.

4

The first inquiry is, whether we have an institution of servitude now existing in the State. This must be answered in the affirmative, if the opinions referred to contain the law of the State, or are to be adopted as the law of the State. If such be the law, we not only have such an institution, but it is a thing capable of extension and expansion without limit. The service, in these cases, was a single day in the year, but the principle would just as well sustain a claim for every day in the year : The money or things in kind provided for, are comparatively small in amount. But, by the same rule, if the owner of lands should covenant to serve three hundred and sixty-five days in the year, or should covenant to pay as a tribute, all he could raise, or by any means acquire, and should covenant for his heirs and assgins, every succeeding owner of the same lands, would be liable to perform the covenant. The covenantor might except himself from the obligations of his covenants, by fixing the time they were to begin. It is easy to perceive, that by adopting a rule which allows one man to bind another, and one generation of men to bind all other generations, you have an institution of servitude likely to take to itself giant proportions.

The second inquiry relates to the assumed origin of the institution. The facts relied upon, stated in a general manner, are as follows ; Some seventy years ago, certain contracts were made by men, of course, long since dead, and with whom the defendants had neither relation nor connection. Those contracts were, in form and effect, conveyances in fee from the one party, with an agreement by the other, to perform a day's service, and deliver an annual tribute of wheat and hens as the price or consideration of the conveyance. The language of the covenants embraced the heirs and assigns. The defendants, fifty years or more after, became owners of the same lands.

Those are the facts upon which you are held to service, and upon which the Courts assume to establish an institution of servitude.

The subject, in its servile phase, is of modern date, in this State. The parties who made the contracts, fulfiled them as they did other personal undertakings. Whether they attached to the lands as obligations on their successors in ownership, was a question which could not, and did not arise while they were owners, and was consequently postponed until a later period. It is not much, if any, over a quarter of a century, since the servile aspect of these contracts began to be pressed upon the attention of the people. It naturally produced excitement and resentment amongst those upon whom it was claimed to fall. They had been educated as freemen in a State which boasted of its free institutions. To submit peaceably, or even passively, to such servile exactions, appeared to them self-degradation.

Great effort was made, by interested parties, to create in the public mind the impression that the repugnance manifested was the result of bad faith and a general disposition to repudiate honest debts, and defraud honest creditors. A more unfounded slander was never attempted. The frauds and bankruptcies which have sometimes reduced competence to want, and made paupers of the widows and the fatherless, have not sprung from that source.

There were extraneous considerations which deepened the resent-

ment of the people. Such obligations could not have been imposed
in England. There was a statute existing there as early as 1290,
which made them impossible. It was claimed that the people of this
State, in their general adoption of English laws, had omitted that
statute; and the omission was credited to the influence of the large
landholders.

While the system was denounced by men prominent in authority, by
governors and by the legislature, as inconsistent with the genius of
our government and prejudicial to the public welfare, active measures
were put in operation to rid the state of the admitted evil. But before they were brought to a final result, the subject came before the
Court of Appeals, and that court unanimously decided that the English statute of 1290 making the creation of feudal servitude an im-
possibility, had been embodied in our act concerning tenures passed
in 1787; that it "put an end to all feudal tenure between one citizen
and another, and substituted in its place a tenure between each landholder and the people in their sovereign capacity;" and "placed the
law of this state, in respect to the question in controversy, on the
same footing on which the law of England now stands and has stood
since the reign of Edward the First." (2 Selden, 504-5).

Thus in about a dozen years after the contest began, it was finally
decided that feudal tenures, and of course, feudal servitude, did not
and could not exist in the state, by conveyances in fee made since
July 4, 1776. On a subsequent occasion, the same court reiterated
the same decision, and extended it so as to embrace the colonial period alike with the state. (19 N. Y. 76).

The decision of that point put an end to all such claims, so far as
the laws of the state were concerned. This was conceded by counsel of the claimants. They never have, personally or by counsel,
contended that they could enforce their demands against third parties
upon any other theory than that of feudal tenures. That theory was
pronounced by the court untenable; and it follows, that if we have
an institution of servitude, by which defendants in such cases can be
held legally liable, it has sprung from other than a feudal source.

The next epoch of the subject began in 1858. The claimants having sold and assigned in fee, had no lands and no estate in lands.
The law was so clearly settled against them, that no lawyer off the
bench could design a theory which he dare put forth as an advocate
in their favor. They were more fortunate in finding an advocate on
the bench. By that means, the Supreme Court of the third judicial
district, was induced to direct its energies to uphold the system from
the crushing effects of the decision of 1852. They could find nothing
in the common law to help; nothing in the laws of any state or na-
tion, except our own. So they proclaimed. (See 27 Barb., 164),

Chapter 98 of the laws of 1805—passed years after the contracts
sued upon were made—was the particular act selected.

The selection and application of that act, were extraordinary; but
the manner of making it work out the result, was more extraordinary than the application itself. We give that part of their labors
in their own language: " Applying an act, enabling grantees of reversions to hold certain rights and enforce certain remedies, by reason
of being assignees of reversions, it, of necessity, makes the lessor's

interest in such a lease, — as well in his own hands, as in those of his assignees, *pro hac vice* equivalent to a reversion." And "being subsequent (as was the act it amended) to the law concerning tenures, it is, if, and so far as, repugnant to that law, a repealing act, even without the express words, ' any law,' &c." (27 Barb., 152).

The plain meaning of this is, that the contracts sued upon were, when made, assignments, by force of the express provisions of the statute concerning tenures; that subsequently, and by the retroaction of the statute of 1805, the assignments were changed to leases.

Had the statute clearly expressed such an intention, no one will deny, but that it would have been a flagrant attempt, on the part of the legislature, to exercise an extraordinary power; no less than making contracts to differ in meaning and effect from what the parties had made them. Of course, if the legislature could change an assignment into a lease, they could change a lease into an assignment. If they could create the relations of landlord and tenant where those relations did not exist, they could dissolve those relations where they did exist.

But the statute of 1805 expressed no such intention. No such meaning can be deduced from the language. It merely gave certain rights of action to the grantees of reversions of leases in fee. The language is too explicit for cavil. It did not include assignments, nor reach other parties than grantees of reversions. Thus by the very terms of the statute, it could not apply to the plaintiff, nor to the contracts sued upon.

It was not the statute which did the work. An act of the legislature which should declare all assignments leases, or all leases assignments, with a view to create obligations where none existed, or discharge them where they did exist, would be so obvious an outrage that no court would dare to give to it effect. The statute was used only as a mask. The mode of construction demonstrates this. "Law is the perfection of reason," says the judge : (27 Barb., 143) and he proceeds to demonstrate his maxim upon the materials before him. The first thing was to assume that the legislature intended to apply the statute to assignments, and to parties other than grantees of reversions; and, consequently, that the court were not at liberty to refuse so to apply it. But the language of the statute, by reason of its inaptitude, would not apply. They make that the fortunate feature for their purpose. They could not change the language of the act, and must therefore change the thing to which they were forced to apply it. In other words, as the legislature had not fitted the statute to the thing, the court must fit the thing to the statute. Hence, " of necessity," as they reason, they are forced to " make" an *assignment* into a *lease*, and a thing which is not a *reversion* and bears no resemblance to a *reversion*, into a *pro hac vice* equivalent to a reversion.

This mode of construing statutes by the rule of contraries, and upon the maxim that " law is the perfection of reason," will be more readily understood by the common mind, on applying it to familiar objects. For example: We have statutes which, according to their express language, apply only to dogs. Suppose some one could profit by applying the same statutes to horses, instead of dogs. He has only to convince the judges that the legislature, in using the word

7

dogs, really meant horses. It would be a task of no greater apparent
difficulty then to convince them that in using the word lease, the
legislature meant assignment. The conviction once produced, no matter how, or by what means, all the rest would come easy. The judges
would find no difficulty in adapting their formula of logic to meet the
case. They have only to say, "applying a statute to a horse, which
by its language applies only to a dog, of necessity *makes* the horse a
dog, or — which is the same thing — *pro hoc vice*, equivalent to a
dog." And who doubts that the horse would become just as good a
dog as the assignment would a lease!

This theory of making law by a forced process of reasoning, passed
in review before the Court of Appeals in 1859, and received the sanc-
tion of that court in an elaborate opinion, which has been reported
(19 N. Y., 68). That court, in commenting on the statute of 1805,
declared that it placed " the assignees of both parties upon grants in
fee, upon the same footing which was occupied by the assignees of the
parties to a lease for life or years " (19 N. Y., 92).

There was only one point in the argument of the court below,
which they sought to strengthen. It might be contended that leases
in fee did exist here before the institution of the state government.
The Court of Appeals so held in 1852 (2 Selden, 503). That being
so, the court seemed to have feared that the statute of 1805 might
have a legitimate application, and thus weaken that law of "necessity," by which they sought to force it into an illegitimate connection.
" It was in part to furnish an answer to that suggestion," says the
learned judge, " that I have taken the pains to show that there was
never a period in this state when conveyances in fee between individuals created a tenure " (19 N. Y., 84).

With that point thus fortified, the learned author of that opinion
expressed his unqualified conviction that the intent of the legislature
to embrace assignments was " plain and certain;" and, that effect
must be given to that intent, though the language was " incongruous."
(19 N. Y., 84).

The intended force of that point is evident. There being no leases
in fee in the state, to which the statute could apply, in obedience to
its language, it must be applied to assignments in disobedience to its
language; and that application, " of necessity," changed all assignments to leases.

The cogency of this point also will be more impressive by apylying
it to the supposed case before put. Thus, could it be shown with
equal certainty that there was not a dog in the state, and never had
been, and never could be, then the statutes in regard to dogs would
just as clearly have been intended for horses, and the court just as
stringently coerced to so apply it. Hence it would need no argument,
according to the judicial dialectics, to show that the whole equine
race would be changed to canine, and therefore subject to all the
muzzle-wearing, sheep-killing penalties of the statute.

That was all there was of the triumph of " the feudal lords " by
the decisions of 1858 and 1859. They had not acquired proprietor-
ship in the lands; they had only what their friends on the bench called a " *pro hac vice* equivalent." In the language of the court, they
were by those decisions, based expressly upon the statute of 1805,

placed on the *same footing* of the owners of lands who had tenants under them for life or years. It was an easy matter to say so, but quite another to realize it. There were two parties to that arrangement. The courts had seen but one. They could not give to one party without taking from the other. The court overlooked that feature of the case. The losing parties did not.

Moreover, those decisions were not placed before the public in a way to command a great degree of respect. There were weak points in the argument, so obvious that they could not escape observation.

In the first place there was a decisive admission that the plaintiffs were not what they pretended to be, that is, they were not the reversioners of the lands with tenants under them. Had they been so, the task of the court was an easy one, for then no defence was pretended. By trying to get up an equivalent for the reversion, they admitted that the plaintiffs had not the reversion, and thereby admitted, as a question of law ,the other point of the defence, that the plaintiffs not having the reversion, could not recover; for if that was not true, there was no necessity for contriving something equivalent to a reversion to supply the want.

In the second place, the manner of making the "equivalent" was not one calculated to command the respect of an intelligent people. It was the first time that a court had ever assumed that a statute meant just the opposite of what its language expressed. And then the mode of what they call "the perfection of reason," by which they assumed "of necessity" to change one thing to another, has had no parallel.

At the next session of the legislature an act was passed declaring "that the act of 1805 and its subsequent reënactments shall not apply to deeds of conveyance in fee made before the passage of that act, nor to such deeds hereafter to be' made " (Laws of 1860, p. 675).

The Legislature uundoubtedly acted under the belief, that if the Courts were relieved from applying the act of 1805, they would be relieved from the necessity of *making* an *assignment* into a *lease*, and of *placing* those who owned no lands on the "same footing" with those who did own.

The Supreme Court of the third district refused to be relieved, and reiterated the argument of the 27, Barb. before cited, about making "*Legislative reversions*," and "*Statute reversions*" in order to enforce the claims of the plaintiffs. They assumed that there was no liability of the defendants, except as it was created by the Act of 1805; and that the repeal of that act would destroy the liability, by destroying the "Legislative reversion," which that act created. Hence they would not believe that the legislature meant what they expressly declared ; and, moreover, they denied that the Legislature had the constitutional right to pass an act of such meaning. According to their logic the Legislature could create a liability, but could not remove it. But there was nothing new in the argument, and nothing which has since commanded any attention from the parties or their counsel, or the Court above. We need, therefore, bestow no more space upon that decision. The leading opinion will be found reported in 33 Barb. 136.

Next in order, come the opinions hereto annexed. We do not in-

tend, in this communication, to review them at length. We annex
the points on both sides, as made on the argument, which will enable you to understand the questions which were really presented; and
by reading the opinions, you can judge for yourselves what questions
the Court have omitted to notice, what they have passed upon, and
how they have done it. There are only a few peculiarities character-
ising the opinions to which we shall now direct your attention.

You will perceive that the opinions and theory of the Supreme
Court command no respect from the Court of Appeals—not so much
as a notice. The Court of Appeals sweeps away the foundation of
that theory, by deciding that the Act of 1805 was repealed by the
Act of 1860; and they furnish no substitute or equivalent in the place
of it. On the contrary, by formally declaring it to be a settled proposition, that the contracts sued upon were not *leases*, but *assignments*,
and could not operate as *leases*, that they left in the grantor neither
any reversion nor a possibility of reverter, they stripped the plaintiffs as naked as they were born, of all right to rents and services as
against the defendants. Had the Court taken the trouble to examine
the points and authorities, they would have given judgment for the
defendants. They could only have failed to perceive the nude condition of the plaintiffs by shutting their eyes, or failing to look. The
plaintiffs are not so inattentive to the nakedness in which they were
left. They repudiate, as you will know, the positions of the Court
and persist in calling the contracts leases, and keeping up their pre-
tensions about ownership of the "soil." The reason which gov-
erns them is obvious. Placed before the public in the plight where
the Court have left them, they foresee their inevitable failure to sustain the system of servitude by which they seek to profit. They understand, what the judges seem not to have been conscious of, that
there is always, in the rear of all courts, a public opinion, upon which
their decisions must rest. For example, should the Court hold one
man liable to pay another's debts, because the two parties were resi-
dents of the same town, or the same house, the judgment would be
so obviously contrary to law, that it could not be enforced. Such a
court would be driven from office by general consent.

The rent-claimants evidently regard the last decision of the Court
of Appeals as of that character; and consequently they ignore the
doctrine therein proclaimed. The practical question forced upon you,
is whether you will regard it with more respect than they do.

To determine that question, you must place yourselves upon the
stand-point fixed by the Court, and see whether, starting from that
point, the laws of the State have fixed your position in society as
persons held to service. If they have, you are liable. If they have
not, you are not liable.

The first thing is to see what light, if any, the Court has thrown
upon the subject. In the first place, they resolved that you were persons held to service. But they had previously determined that you
were tenants in fee, holding by a tenure immediately of the State;
and that the plaintiffs were only the assignees of certain covenants
made seventy years ago, by persons, now dead, on the occasion of
their purchasing and taking an assignment of estates in fee. In other

words, they were assignees of the purchase money covenants from vendees to vendors on the sale and conveyance of lands in fee. The question of law was, therefore, whether purchase money covenants from a vendee to his vendor on purchase of lands in fee made in 1790 attached as a servitude to the estate purchased. No one dare claim the affirmative of that proposition. Even when such a covenant is secured by mortgage on the lands purchased, a subsequent purchaser incurs no personal liability to pay it. (See authority on p. 26).

The court in the opinions annexed admit the negative of that proposition: and they meet the point, by saying that it is not true, as claimed by defendants' counsel, that the covenants were purchase money covenants. (See p. 56). If they are wrong in that denial, they are of course wrong in holding you bound to service by the contracts of men dead before you were born. Let us test the truth or falsehood of the denial by their own decision. They have decided that the covenantors purchased the land, and that the covenants were the consideration price of such purchase. If they are not purchase money covenants, what are they? Their phraseology is peculiar. They do not say that the covenants are rent covenants; they only say that they *are as clearly rent* as they would have been if the covenantor had covenanted for other lands previously owned by him to secure the same purchase money. They might. with as much propriety have said, they were as clearly rent as though made in consideration of the purchase of a yoke of oxen. With as much truth, they might have declared any other debt incurred by the covenantors to be a debt for rent, and that you were, therefore, liable to pay it. The lawyer who mistakes such a thing for rent, should consult the dictionaries, and failing to learn better there, he should go to his law books. We would commend his attention particularly to Hope v. Booth, 20 Eng. Com. Law Rep., 574, and Parmenter v. Webber, 8 Taunton, 593; or if he discards English reports, look at Sackett v. Barnum. 22 Wen., 605. He will find that, even where parties have agreed on the purchase of lands, "that the relation of landlord and tenant shall and does henceforth exist between the parties to all intents and purposes, and that the parties of the first part may collect and recover all moneys becoming or to become due on the contract by distress or otherwise, as for so much rent due," it has been decided that the payments are not rent. Upon such an agreement the court, Bronson J., (22 Wen., 607), said that, "the several payments wh ch the vendee was to make were not a rent or return for the temporary enjoyment of the land; they were not reserved out of the annual profits by way of recompense or retribution for the possession of the property, but they were a part of the consideration for the sale — the price of the land itself — with the addition of interest, because the payments were postponed to future periods. On default of payment, the parties have stipulated for a remedy by distress, as for so much rent due. Whatever may be the legal effect of this agreement. as between the parties to it, I think they could not, as against third persons, turn the price of the land itself into rent." Those were stronger cases in that direction than the ones before the court. They were passing upon contracts, which did not assume to create any relations of landlord and tenant. No such words were inserted therein. *Again,* the people are informed that " If the relation of landlord and tenant between the parties were necessary, it would not be difficult to show that that relation exists in this case.''

Let us examine that point. The court have decided that the contract is an *assignment* and not a *lease*. Now will any member of that court show how they can make the relation of landlord and tenant result from a contract of assignment? There are quite a number of decisions of our courts in the way of such a result. We have already cited one, Sackett v. Barnum. And if there can be any rule so well settled by the authorities as to be beyond question, this is one, namely, that the relations of landlord and tenant can not be created except by a lease. All the elementary writers agree upon this point. There are no exceptions. We will cite a few of them:

1 Platt on Leases. p. 19; Taylor's Lan. & Ten., §16, 426, 431; 2 Prest. on Conveyancing. 124; 2 Platt on Leases, p. p. 9, 102.

It has been repeatedly decided by our courts. that the relation of landlord and tenant can be created only by a lease. Sims v. Humphrey, 4 Denio, 185, 187, 188 ; Everston v. Sutton, 5 Wen., 281, 284 ; Roach v. Cosine, 9 Wen. 227, 232 ; Williams v. Bigelow, 11 How. Pr. Rep., 83. 88; Benjamin v. Benjamin. 1 Selden Rep., 383.

Those are some of the difficulties in the shape of authority which the court will encounter when they attempt to show the relation of landlord and tenant between the parties to this controversy.

In another part of their argument, the court say, the covenant is. " not a covenant in gross or a mere chose in action,'' but a covenant real, and, therefore, you are bound as persons being held to service, To prove that, they gravely cite Stevenson v. Lumbard. 2 East., 576. That was an action upon a lease for 31 years, to recover rents according to the covenants of the lessee, by the party owning the reversion. There was no doubt of the covenant being real, because the covenantee had the reversion. and the covenant belonged to him while he owned the reversion, and no longer. But in the case before the court, the covenantee had no estate in the lands to which the covenant could attach. How, then, could the covenant be real as distinguished from personal?

But this was not a new question. In 1852, the same Court of Appeals declared a similar covenant in just such an instrument to be " a mere right or chose in action.'' (2 Selden, 506). They repeated the same thing in 1859 (19 N. Y.. 91). The elementary writers are uniformly the same way. Williams on Real Property. pp. 265, 273; Watkins on Conveyancing, 173, 4; Gilbert on Rents, pp. 15, 18; and other elementary works.

The court admit that the defendants are not liable unless they are in *privity* of *estate* with the plaintiff. And to prove that they are in privity, they say : "It is settled both in this state and in England, that an assignment creates such a *privity* of estate between the assignee and the lessee.'' And they cite three cases, namely : Ards v. Watkins, Cro. & Elis. 63; Allen v. Bryan, 5 B. & C., 512. and Stevenson v. Lombard. 2 East. 576. The first cited case was upon a lease for 30 years ; the second on a lease for 14 years ; and the last is the case we have already noticed, upon a lease for 31 years. Are not these citations astounding ?

Again: The court says that it was contended by the defendant that
tenure was necessary to make a covenant run with the land as a burden; and by way of refutation, they deny the truth of the proposition, and cite certain cases in regard to easements. By referring to
the points on the part of the defendants (page 20), you will perceive that the court were utterly at fault in regard to the fact. The defendant did not contend that tenure was necessary, and he cited the
'very cases, as to easements, which the court cite. But the cases, as
to easements, would not help the plaintiff, because the contracts in
question were just as far from creating easements as they were from
creating tenure.

Those are fair specimens of the whole judicial argument. It is difficult to understand the confusion of ideas, which cites from cases
where the relations of landlord and tenant confessedly exist, to sustain actions where such relations are decided not to exist. It is like
declaring a man to be free, and then attempting to show that he is a
person held to service, by citing cases where slaves have been so held.
So much for their common law argument.

But there was one point on the part of the defence, and it was the
one most pressed upon the court, which they have not attempted to
meet; and that was the statute in force when the contracts were
made, which provided that every purchaser of an estate in fee should
hold the lands so purchased "of the same fee, by the same services
and customs by which the person or persons making such sale or
alienation, before held the same lands or tenements." (See the points,
page 42.)

Here was an express statute, providing that no one should be held
to service by reason of becoming a purchaser of lands in fee. It was
a copy of an act which has been in force in England for more than
five centuries. It was enacted for the very purpose of preventing the
imposition of rents and services upon estates in fee when such estates
were transfered from one person to another. That it accomplished
that purpose fully and effectually, has never been denied. Even Mr.
Sugden has not expressed an opinion that it " ought " to be otherwise.
That statute was a part of these contracts, and must be read as a
part. Neither legislatures nor courts have the power to change it.
Why then have the court passed that point in silence? Why have
they disregarded its effects? Those are questions which you have a
right to put, and which you should repeat until they are satisfactorily
answered.

The opinion in the ejectment case, first admits all the points of the
defendant, which you will find at p. 26, et seq. But to sustain the judgment, the court rely solely upon a case which was decided in England
200 years ago. (Jemot v. Cooly). The facts of that case were
as follows: On the 20th of July, 1651, one Drake was the owner in
fee of certain lands and borrowed 6,000l. of one Bovey, and to secure it, granted a rent-charge of 420l. a year. The grant contained
this agreement: "And the said Drake doth covenant and grant to
the said Sir Ralph Bovey, that if the rent be arrear above twenty
days after any day of payment, that then the said Sir Ralph Bovey and
his heirs and assigns may enter into the lands and receive the profits,
until he shall be satisfied of the arrears."

The court in that case held that " Here the thing granted is only
a power and not the term itself, and it is as a distress; but this power
produces a real effect, when the grantee hath entered he hath only a
pernancy of the profits ; for he cannot cut trees, or pull down houses,
and if he doth, trespass lies against him, as against him who abuses
a distress."

The court have furnished a severe commentary upon this decision,
in their opinion in the Reid case. Referring therein to the Ball case,
they say that case cannot be sustained without showing the existence
of the relations of landlord and tenant. Now they not only show
that no such relation exists, but rely solely upon a case where there
was no pretence of such a relation. Moreover in the case before them,
there was no such contract as existed in Jemot agt. Cooly.

By reading the points of the defendant in connection with the
opinion you will be able to understand that the decision of the court
violates not only the plain provisions of our statutes, but disregards
all the material rules as to ejectment which have been heretofore
adopted by the courts. Taking the case of Jemot agt. Cooly as the
standard relied upon, and the plaintiff would have no right to put any
one off the premises. He could only enter and cultivate and take
his wheat and fat fowls, and then he must retire from the possession,
or he wonld be a trespasser. The introduction of such an action to
our practice is novel to our laws, and will necessarily give rise to many
new questions. Heretofore, in order to sustain ejectment, the plaintiff must first have proved title in himself to the premises claimed, and
second, wrongful possession in the defendant. Under the present
ruling of the court the plaintiff must first prove title in the
defendant to the premises claimed, and second that the defendant
is rightfully in possession; and then a contract by some previous
owner creating a personal obligation, and to secure its fulfillment, a
further agreement that the covenantee, in case of failure, may enter
and have the premises as his own by way of forfeiture.

It has been accepted doctrine, that property can no more be made
the subject of forfeiture, than liberty or life. Some of you may re-
member the decision of the same court regarding the sale of intoxi-
cating liquors, and declaring a statute unconstitutional and void, because it imposed forfeiture as a penalty, Have individuals greater
power to regulate the incidents of property than the legislature?
Where do the court get power to take from one man who owns, and
give to another who does not own? Have they authority to take a
man's property more than his life? And how much respect would be
paid to the judgment of the court, which should authorise a plaintiff
to take the defendant's life?

These are practical questions, which are forced upon you; and they
involve your freedom or your servitude. The manner in which you
shall meet them will determine your lot, whether you are to be classed
as freemen or marked as slaves.

In conclusion, let us sum up the progress of this contest. Rents
and services were demanded of you by the Van Rensselaers, on the
ground that they were your landlords and you their tenants. They
assumed to base those relations upon certain conveyances in fee,
which they claimed were leases in perpetuity. The reversion, which

would have remained had they been leases, they claimed to have derived by will from the grantor, and that, thus, they were the owners of "the soil," and your landlords.

We advised you that the conveyances were not leases, but assignments. You resisted their demands on that ground alone. If you were right in that position, it was conceded that you were not liable. If you were wrong, you did not deny your liability. That was substantially the whole issue as it was submitted to the court by the parties and their counsel. In 1859, as before shown, the courts decided against you, solely upon the ground that the statute of 1805 had changed the deeds of assignment to deeds of lease. That statute was then repealed, and the court, thus relieved, have decided the only question of law, in dispute between the parties and their counsel, in your favor, without ambiguity or qualification. *There was therefore no ground left upon which the court could legally affirm the judgment.* It is not only unsustained by law, but in conflict with the express provisions of the statutes of the state.

You will naturally ask whether you have any remedy against such action of the judiciary.

If you were the tenants of a responsible individual, and thus disturbed in your rights, you would have a 'direct remedy against your landlord. But you are the tenants of the state, as all other landowners are, and have no landlord to fall back upon except the state. You can not sue the state. But it does not follow that you have no remedy. Judges are only the official agents of the state. They have no power to substitute as law their whims or sympathies for the success of any particular class of claimants, nor to change the fundamental rules of law.

If it occasionally happens that such is the case, it is generally corrected by subsequent decisions. Wrong can have no permanent success. Truth is sure of triumph in the end. In your case, it is not possible for the court to give such a judgment honestly, and persist in it. after their attention is directed to its injustice and absurdity. There is, therefore, reason to hope that the same court will correct their errors, on a further presentation of the questions.

But, however that may be, the legislative department of the government, which has the power to make the laws, has also the power to see that they are properly administered. It is the only way in which the state can be called on as landlord, to protect you in your possessions, against the aggressions of strangers to you, when such aggressions receive the countenance of the courts.

You applied to the legislature in 1860 for relief, and the statute of 1805, upon which the courts charged your liability, was promptly repealed.

Now, that your liability is charged upon different ground, while it is decided, without equivocation, that the statute of 1787 is, and ever since that time has been, in full force, whereby it was made impossible to impose the burdens and services in question, you have no reason to apprehend, that the legislature will not come, with equal promptness, to your relief.

COLVIN & BINGHAM.

ALBANY, December, 1863.

In the Court of Appeals.

STEPHEN VAN RENSSELAER, *Respondent, agt.* HENRY BONESTEEL, *Appellant.*

Points for Appellant ; Statement of the Case.

This was an action for the breach of certain covenants made by
one Lodewick Bonesteel in 1794. Judgment for plaintiff on demurrer to the complaint, Oct., 1855. Affirmed at General Term 1858
(fol. 53). The ground of demurrer that the complaint did not state
facts sufficient to constitute a cause of action. The facts alleged are
that Stephen Van Rensselaer, now deceased, sold and conveyed certain lands to the said Lodewick Bonesteel in 1794. and the said Lodewick Bonesteel covenanted to pay ten bushels of wheat yearly: and
the defendant had become owner of the same estate before 1848, and
remained the owner in a part of the said premises; and plaintiff had
become the owner of the covenants.

The plaintiff claimed that the defendant was liable for a part of the
ten bushels of wheat for every year he was the owner of part of the
lands (fols. 6 to 25).

The question was whether the defendant was liable. This court
in a similar case sustained tne judgment on the ground that the statute of 1805, in regard to grantees of reversions, retroacted upon
the contract and made the defendant liable. The question now to
be presented is, whether that act construed to create the liability, was
within tne constitutional limits of the legislature.

Points.

I. The liability of the defendant must rest upon principles entirely
aside from any which relate to the liability of the covenantor upon
his own covenant. The latter would be liable by reason of his privity of contract. The former was not in privity of contract and could
not be made liable unless he was in privity of estate. But it being
decided that the instrument containing the covenant did not create a
new estate, but only assigned a preëxisting one, there was no privity
of estate in connection with the covenants, when the contract was
made. The covenanting parties were in no relation to each other,
except that of vendor and vendee, and confessedly the covenants of
the latter could not fall as a personal burden upon subsequent purchasers (27 Barb., 173). Then came chapter 98 of the laws of 1805,
which has been held to create the liability. The theory is, that the
retroaction of the statute upon the annual payment made it " equivalent to a reversion " (27 Barb., 15"); " made it for all purposes of
transfer and the rights to enforcement by law, *a reversion* "(33 Barb.,
137). That " being subsequent to the law concerning tenure, it was,
so far as repugnant to that law, a repealing act (27 Barb., 152), and
placed " the assignees of both parties upon grants in fee, where a rent
was reserved, upon the same footing which was occupied by the assignees of the parties to a lease for life or years (19 N. Y., 92), and
thus changed the assignment to a lease, thereby establishing the

same feudal relations between the parties, both original and derivative, as might have been established had the feudal law been in force
as it existed in England before 1290. (*Van Rensselaer v, Heidon*,
decided *Sept. Term of this court*, 1860).

II. The statute of 1805, with such an application and construction
impairs the obligation of the contract by which the estate in fee was
held of the state, and is, therefore, so far, void, because in conflict
with the provisions of the constitution of the United States, which
prohibits a state from passing any law impairing the obligation of
contracts (art. 1, sec. 10, sub. 1).

First. The estate in fee held by the defendant is the same which
belonged to the senior Van Rensselaer, and which he transferred to
Lodewick Bonesteel in 1794. That estate was the executed contract
of the state, that the grantee and his heirs and assigns might enjoy
the possession of the premises forever. The obligations of that contract still continue. *De Peyster v. Michael*, 2 Selden, 467. *Van
Rensselaer v. Hayes*, 19 N. Y., 68.

Second. It was a contract within the provision of the constitution.
This proposition has been repeatedly decided. *Fletcher v. Peck*, 6
Cranch R., 87, 136. *New Jersey v. Wilson*, 7 id., 164. *Dartmouth
College v. Woodward*, 4 Wheaton, 656.

The rule of those cases has been uniformly adopted and is placed
beyond question. *Story on the Constitution*, § 1376.

Third. The defendant held the premises as the assignee of that
contract, of which the state was the party of the first part. 2 *Selden*, 504, 5; 19 N. Y., 73, 4.

And if liable in this action, his liability arises from that fact. But
that contract did not require the payment sought; and if the act of
1805 was intended to impose such a requirement, it would impair the
obligations of that contract which still continue. *The People v. Platt*,
17 John., 195.

In this case, the state granted lands in 1784 to one Platt, in fee,
the premises granted including the Saranac river. In 1786, Platt
erected a dam across the river near its mouth. In 1801, an act was
passed requiring the owners of dams to alter them, so as to allow
salmon to pass. The statute was reenacted in 1813. In 1817, the
defendant's dam not being conformed to the requirements of the statute, was indicted as a nuisance. It was held that the statutes, so far
as they affected the r ghts of Platt and his assigns to the Saranae,
within the limits of the grant to him, impaired the obligations of the
contract under which he held, and were unconstitutional and void
(see pp. 215, 16).

This case followed *Fletcher v. Peck*, and *New Jersey v. Wilson*,
before cited. In the last, there had been a grant in fee of lands with
the provision that they should be exempt from taxation. It was held
they could not be subjected to taxation by a repeal of the provision.

The same doctrine was held in *Atwater v. Woodbridge*, 6 Con., 230,
and in *Osborn v. Humphrey*, 7 Con., 341. *Story on the Constitution*,
§ 1391.

The rule of those cases applies to this. The defendant here is
claimed to be liable because of his holding an estate in fee, immediately of the state, in other words, because he holds as the assignee of

a contract of which the state is party of the first part. The defendant has no connection with any other contract, and that contract imposes no such obligation as claimed in this action. The statute, therefore, which should impose this additional obligation, would impair the obligation of that contract.

III. The statute of 1805, construed to make the defendant liable upon the covenants of Lodewick Bonesteel in the deed of 1794, would impair the obligation of that contract and would be, therefore, void.

First. That indenture did not create a new tenure or new estate. In other words it was not a contract for the holding of the lands, but the assignment of the contract by which they were before held of the state. It was the ordinary executed contract of bargain and sale by the one party, with a covenant by the other, as vendee, for the purchase price. As the common law existed here when the contract was made, this covenant did not run with the land. 19 N. Y., 73, 4; 27 Barb., 173.

Second. At that time there was a statute applicable to the indenture, which provided that every purchaser of an estate in fee should hold the lands or tenements so purchased "of the same fee, by the same services and customs by which the person or persons making such gift, sale or alienation, before held the same lands or tenements," (I R. L,. 70, sec. 1). If nothing else had been in the way, the statute would have prevented that contract from imposing the covenant of Lodewick Bonesteel as a service or condition by which the estate purchased was afterwards to be held.

Third. The contract must be interpreted and its character and effect determined by the laws of the state in force and applicable when the contract was made; and the statute of 1805 and its re-enactments, so far as intended to change those laws and thus change the character and effect of the contract, impaired its obligation, and were therefore in conflict with the constitution and void.

See authorities cited under second point, and Proprietors of the Kennebeck Purchase v. Laboree. 2 Maine Rep., 275.

In this case the statute had changed the common law rule as to disseisin. Held it could not have a retroactive effect because the constitution secures the citizen against the retroactive effect of legislation upon his property; and, that the statute retroacts which creates a new obligation or imposes a new duty (pp. 287, 290-5). *Ogden v. Sanders*, 12 Wheaton, 259; *Sturges v. Crowninshield*, 207; *Mather v. Bush*, 16 John., 233; *Bronson v. Kinsie*, 1 How. U S., 319; *Planters' Bank v. Sharp*, 6 id., 210, 11; *Varick's Ex'rs v. Briggs*, 22 Wend., 543; *Lessee of Gantly v. Ewing*, 3 How. U. S., 707.

Fourth. The legislature could not make the defendant liable for a debt contracted before the act.

This has been held in regard to a statute giving towns a right to sue paupers for moneys expended in their support. It could not embrace expenses incurred before the statute. *Medfor v. Learned*, 16 Mass., 216.

The same doctrine has been held as to statutes declaring stockholders of corporations individually liable. It could not make them liable for debts contracted before the act. *Coffin v. Rich.*, 45 Maine R., 507.   2

IV. Construe the indenture by the laws of the state in force when it was made in 1794, and the defendant was not liable.

·First. Our laws then in force bearing upon this case, were precisely like the laws of England. 2 Selden, 504, 5: 19 N. Y., 76.

Second. By those laws it was necessary that there should be either a privity of contract, or a privity of estate between the parties in order to make one party the debtor of the other.

In McKercher v. Hawley. 16 John., 292. Spencer. Ch. J., said: "If there be no privity of contract or estate, most certainly an action could not be maintained."

In Webb v. Russell, 3 Term Rep., 403. Lord Kenyon stated the rule thus: "It is not sufficient that a covenant is concerning the land, but in order to make it run with the land, there must be a privity of estate between the covenanting parties."

The same rule is adopted in Bally v. Wells, Wilmot's Notes, 344; Allen v. Culver, 3 Denio, 297; Dolph v. White, 2 Kernan, 301.

Third. "Privity of estate is the result of tenure; it subsists by virtue of the relation of landlord and tenant." 2 Platt on Leases, p. 351; Bouvier's L. Dic.; Sugden on Vendors and Purchasers, pp. 713, 14; Chambers' L. and Ten., 479, 80; Taylor's Lan. and Ten., §436; Woodfall's Lan. and Ten., p. 214, and p. 580, 7th ed., and all the other elementary writers upon this subject.

See also the cases cited under the second proposition of this point.

The cases holding that the undertenant is not liable upon the lessee's covenants are in point. They are put upon the ground that there is neither privity of contract nor privity of estate between such parties. Taylor's Lan. and Ten. §448; Holfor v. Hatch, Doug. R., 183; Quackenbush v. Clark, 12 Wend., 555; Cole v. Marquand, 2 Hill, 449.

V. Between the vendor and the vendee of an estate, there is no privity of estate such as is required to fasten the obligations of the covenants of the vendee upon subsequent purchasers. They are privies in estate, that is, the estate has passed immediately from the one to the other. But this is a kind of privity, which, in the language of Coke, " is ever immediate " (Co. Litt., 271, a). It cannot be transferred so as to exist between their assignees, making them vendor and vendee. Lessor and lessee are also privies in estate; but that kind of privity between them " is ever immediate," and cannot be transferred so that their respective assignees will be to each other lessor and lessee. But there is between lessor and lessee another kind of privity, to wit, a privity by tenure. The right of possession of the lessee is derived from the contract of lease; and that contract attaches itself to the land; to the estate left in the lessor on the one hand, and to the estate created by the instrument itself on the other. The privity so constituted is what is called the privity of estate.

"A lessee, during his occupation. holds both by privity of estate and of contract. His privity of estate depends upon and is co-existent with the continuance of his term. By an assignment he divests himself of this privity and transfers it to his assignee; it remains annexed to the estate, into whose possession soever the lands may pass, and the assignee always holds in privity of estate of the original landlord. The privity of contract, however, is not transmitted to a purchaser, on an assignment by the lessee; for it will, during the whole term, be obligatory on him and his personal representatives, even for breaches after an assignment." Taylor's Lan. and Ten., § 436, and authorities there cited.

The contrary doctrine that privity of estate, as used in the books, is only the privity which exists between vendor and vendee, has no foundation in principle or authority (*See opinion of the court below in this case, fols.* 73–76).

First. As a question of principle, there is this difference between a contract of lease and a contract of assignment. The first is a contract granting the right of possession to certain lands. The second is merely an assignment of that contract by one of the parties. The first fixes the terms and conditions by which the lands are to be held. The second merely assigns the right to so hold to another party.

There is an obvious propriety why the first should attach to the lands. It is indispensable to the existence of an estate, for without the contract there is no estate. The party in possession of lands who denies that he holds by any contract with another person, or with the state. denies the right to hold at all; in effect admits himself to be a trespasser. He is forced by the very exigencies of any legal claim to a rightful possession of lands, to admit the contract under which he holds; and when he has admitted it, he is bound to fulfill the obligations of that contract. He is forced to admit himself to be a party to the contract, because otherwise he has no rights; and while a party he is not at liberty to deny the obligations of the contract.

Hence, whenever the lessor transfers his reversion, his side of the contract of lease passes along with it; and his assignee becomes entitled to all the benefits and subject to all the burdens of the contract of lease, during the time he is assignee, to the same extent and with the same effect, as the lessor. And when the lessee assigns his estate. his side of the contract passes with its benefits and burdens, to his assignee. The respective assignees of the contracting parties become thus mutually bound to each other The one holds possession of lands of the other by the same contract made by their assignors. That connection is what is called a privity of estate; and that is the tie which connects them together, so as to make the one personally liable to the other: and the relations of that tie are called landlord and tenant.

But there is no reason or propriety why the assignment of a lease should attach to the lands, or to the estate assigned. An assignment is not a contract for the possession of the lands. It is only a transfer of such a contract. The respective assignees of a lessor and a lessee, have come to their relations to each other, through different assignments. They may be personally bound to their assignors by their respective contracts of assignment. But as between themselves, there can be no obligations in regard to their respective assignments, because there is no privity between them as to those contracts. Contracts of assignment do not attach to the lands, because neither party on assigning can change the contract by which the lands are held. When a man becomes the owner of an estate by an assignment, he finds the obligation of his position, in the contract of lease which created that estate; and not in the several contracts of assignment, through which it may have come to him. Such was the common law in regard to all estates in lands. Moreover, as to estates in fee, there was a statute in force here in 1794 when the assignment was made upon which this action was brought, which secured the same result by providing that the purchaser should take of the same fee and hold by the same services and customs, by which that fee was before held. 1 R. L., p. 70, sec. 1.

Second. As a question of authority, this difference between a lease and an assignment is well settled. In *Hurd v. Curtis*, 19 Pick Rep., 463, the court, per Wilde J. declared: "There is no exception to the rule, that no covenant will run with the land so as to bind the assignee to perform it, unless there were a *privity of estate* between the covenantor and covenantee."

In other words, the contract must be one granting the right to the possession of lands, and the covenant must relate to the holding of the lands under that contract, and then the assignee of the estate becomes a party to such contract, and is bound by the covenants.

The same principle was applied by the same court in *Morse v. Aldrich*, 19 Pick., 454. There had been a contract or grant of the right to dig muck on the one side, and a covenant in regard thereto on the other. The court held the assignee liable, on the ground that the contract was a grant of a subordinate interest in the lands, and the reversion being left in the grantor, there was a privity of estate between the grantor and grantee of the same kind as exists in the ordinary case of lessor and lessee.

In Smith's Leading Cases, notes to Spencer's case, the English annotator, after reviewing all the English cases upon the subject, says: "Upon the whole, there appears to be no authority for saying that the *burden* of a covenant will run with land in any case, except that of landlord and tenant " (pp. 37-8).

The same distinction between a lease and an assignment, was taken by Lord Brougham in *Keppel v. Bailey*, 2 Mylne & Keene, 517. See also *Randall v. Rigby*, 4 Mees. & Wels., 130; *Taylor v. Owen*, 2 Black Rep., 301, and *Dolph. v. White*, 2 Kernan, 299.

There is no reported case or elementary work which denies this distinction between a contract of lease and a contract of assignment, except the decision in the court below in this case. This will appear obvious by a reference to what have sometimes been referred to as exceptions.

(1.) The covenant of assurance and warranty by a vendor to the purchaser, the benefit of which is held to so pass with the estate sold, that subsequent purchasers in certain cases, may sue thereupon, is not an exception. It involves no question of *privity of estate*, but only a question of *sameness of estate*. The liability of the covenantor arises from his privity of contract, and the estate sold serves only as the medium, of transmitting the covenant to the subsequent purchaser, and thus placing him in privity of contract with the covenantor. The only question in regard to the estate which can arise in connection with the plaintiff's right to sue in such a case is whether he has the *same* estate which was sold when the covenant was made. The assignee of the covenantor in such a case would not be liable, as in the case of a similar covenant by a lessor for the want of that pri-

vity of estate which is peculiar to a lease. This was so conceded by
this court, except as it was held that the assignee of the covenantor
was made liable to such action by the retroactive effect of the act of
1805. *Van Rensselaer v. Ball*, 19 N. Y., 106.

(2.) The earlier cases in this state. such as *Watts v. Coffin*, 11
John., 495; *Lush v. D,use*, 4 Wend,. 313; *Van Rensselaer v. Bradley*, 3 Denio, 135; *Van Rensselver v. Gallup*,, 5 Denio, 460, were not
exceptions to the rule, Those cases were tried upon the assumption,
that the contracts sued upon were leases and created a privity of
estate. The rule as to privity of estate was expressly stated in 5 Denio, 460.

It is true this court has since held, in similar cases. that the assumption that such instruments were contracts of lease was an error;
that they were contracts of sale or assignment, But does that make
the previous decisions authority that it is immaterial whether they
were so or not? Does it make them authority that the covenants of
a vendee attach to the estate purchased so as to fall as a burden upon
all subsequent purchasers?

The more recent cases, such as *Van Rensselaer v. Smith*, 27 Barb.,
104, are not exceptions, but express authority for the rule as to the
privity of estate which we contend for. They expressly held that
no such privity existed between vendor and vendee (27 Barb., 173);
and they put the liability upon the ground that the statute of 1805
and its reënactments, by its retroaction, had *made* the relation of
landlord and tenant to exist, and thereby created the requisite privity of estate.

(3.) The decisions of other states furnish no exceptions. In Pennsylvania, the courts have held leases in fee to exist on the ground
that the statute *quia emptores* was not a part of the laws of that state.
The case of *Ingersoll v. Sergeant* (1 Whart., 337) is not in conflict
with the other cases. It differs only in more particularly passing
upon the question of the necessity of privity of estate.

McMurphy v. Minot (4 N. H., 251) is not an exception. The
owner of a life estate had leased to the owner of the remainder for
an annual rent. He mortgaged to defendant. The Court held the
mortgagee liable. But no point was made as to privity of estate. The
Court assumed the instrument to be a lease, and held the defendant
as mortgagee to be liable,

(4). The doctrine put forth by Judge Willard, in his work upon
real estate and conveyancing. is not in conflict with this distinction
between a lease and an assignment, but fully concurs with it. He concedes all the distinctions which we contend for: that there must be a
lease, and to make a lease there must be a reversion left in the lessor.
But he contends that actions have been maintained by *calling* assignments leases, and calling the parties thereto lessor and lessee and
landlord and tenant, and then applying the laws of landlord and
tenant with like effect as though the parties were really what they
were called. Willard on Real Estate, &c., pp. 207, 208. 425, 431.

In connection therewith, he claims that there is a principle or cus-
tom in our jurisprudence, whereby the laws can be changed by
changing the phrases used to designate parties and their relations,

without regard to the fact that there is nothing behind those phrases corresponding with them.

The learned author evidently misstated his own theory. It is not a change of the laws which is thus brought about, but a change of the rights of parties, by perverting or misapplying the laws to correspond with this arbitrary use of names.

VI. In conclusion, it is therefore submitted, that the defendant, in seeking to reverse this judgment, is not invoking any change of the laws; because none of the authorities are applicable to sustain it, unless the statute of 1805, with its reënactments, is first made to retroact upon the contracts in question; and when so construed, the statute impairs the obligation of the contract by which the estate in fee was held of the state, as well as the contract by which that estate was assigned to Lodewick Bonesteel in 1794, and is, therefore, unconstitutional and void.

First. That the defendant held the estate in fee under a contract with the state, and not under the contract with Lodewick Bonesteel, is conceded by the court below, in the opinion annexed to the case; and so far that opinion is sustained by the decisions of this court. 2 Selden, 504-5, and 19 N. Y., 73-4.

Second. It is equally well settled, that the state could not, by a statute made after the contract by which the estate in fee was held, change that contract, or impose further obligations upon it, and could not change the character and effect of the contract of 1794, so as to attach its provisions as obligations to the contract by which the estate in fee was held.

Third. That the owner of the estate could not, by an assignment in 1794, change the obligations of the contract under which he held of the state, by adding thereto further obligations, is a rule as old as the common law itself.

1. The English statute *quia emptores*, was founded upon that rule, and moreover, added an express provision, that purchasers of an estate in fee, should continue to hold by the same services and customs as the vendor had before held. Our own legislation, in our statutes and present constitution, has recognized and preserved the same principle.

2. The same rule has been uniformly adopted by the courts. It has never been held that a tenant of an estate, whether in fee, or for life or years, could change the terms of the contract under which the tenancy was held by an agreement with his assignee.

A. BINGHAM,

Of Counsel.

In the Court of Appeals.

STEPHEN VAN RENSSELAER, *Respondent, agt.* JOHN READ, *Appellant.*

Points for Appellant; Statement of the Case.

This was action for breach of the covenants of one George Reed, made in 1789 ; action commenced in July, 1860, and tried January, 1861, at the circuit, and judgment for plaintiff. The questions are presented by a case and bill of exceptions.

The facts relied upon to sustain the judgment, are that S. Van Rensselaer, deceased, in 1789, sold and conveyed certain lands to the said George Reed., and he, in consideration thereof, covenanted to deliver yearly 17½ bushels of wheat, 4 fat fowls and to perform ono day's service with carriage and horses (fols. 8-10); that defendant became the owner of the same estate on the 1st of January, 1840, and continued such owner until the commencement of this action (fol. 46). The plaintiff claimed to acquire the right of action upon the covenants by the will of the covenantee, the clause of the will relied upon being as follows: " I give, devise and bequeath unto my son Stephen, his heirs and assigns, all the residue of my lands, tenements, hereditements and real estate, with the rents, issues and profits thereof, situate in the manor of Rensselaerwyck on the west side Hudson river.

The defendant moved for a nonsuit which was denied, and exception was taken by the defendant (fol. 36, et seq.) Judgment was given for plaintiff for $561.68, to which the defendant excepted.

The questions presented were that the plaintiff was not the grantee of the rent, and had no right of action on the covenants.

That the deed to George Read containing the covenants was not a lease but an assignment, and the covenants did not attach to the lands as a burthen to subsequent purchasers.

That the defendant did not hold the lands under the contract to George Read, but as the tenant in fee of the state, and that chapter 98 of the laws of 1805 did not apply to this case when it was tried, by reason of such application being unconstitutional, and by reason of chapter 396 of the laws of 1860, preventing its application.

The points in the case of *Van Rensselaer agt. Henry Bonesteel* are to be regarded as applying to this case, and in addition thereto the following

Points.

VII. There is another reason in this case why the judgment can not be sustained by force of the act of 1805. Chapter 396 of the laws of 1860, declares that that statute and its reenactments shall not apply to deeds of conveyance in fee made before the 9th of April, 1805. It has been objected to the act of 1860. (33 Barb., 137):

First. That a deed like the one upon which this action is brought was not a conveyance in fee, and, therefore, not within reach of the last named act.

The answer to that objection is, that it is one of the undisputed facts of the case, that the grantor before executing the deed, owned an estate in fee; and it is a point settled by the decision of this court that the entire estate of the grantor was conveyed to the grantee by the effect of the deed (19 N. Y., 68). Hence it can be nothing more nor less than a deed of conveyance in fee. The naming of rents could not make it any less than a conveyance in fee, for even a lease in fee, if there could be one, would be equally a conveyance in fee. But the argument concedes that it was the act of 1805 which changed the instrument from a conveyance in fee; so that, if that act is not applied, the difficulty of applying the act of 1860 will not exist, and the application of the latter act prevents the application of the former.

Second. It is also urged that the statute of 1860 can not be made retroactive for a two-fold reason : (1) because such was not the intention of the legislature; and (2) because the constitution would prevent a retroactive effect.

It is a sufficient answer to the first objection that the statute is made retroactive by its very language, expressly reaching back to deeds made before 1805.

The second objection is equally unfounded. The plaintiff had neither right nor remedy, as against the defendant, except what had been given to him by the act of 1805, and its reënactments. The rule is, that when a right of action has been given by statute, it does not become a vested right until after judgment. and consequently can be taken away by statute at any time before judgment. *Coffin v. Rich*, 45 Maine Rep., 507, 14; *Oriental Bank v. Freese*, 18 Maine Rep., 109; *Butler v. Palmer*. 1 Hill, 329; *Commonwealth v. Hampden*, 6 Pick., 501 ; *Same v. Kimball*, 21 id., 373.

VIII. The defendant was not liable, on the ground that the rent was a rent charge. The covenant to pay did not attach to the estate in the lands as a service or burden thereupon, so as to bind subsequent purchasers. The doctrine that the covenant to pay a rent charge runs with the land so as to bind subsequent purchasers has no support in the authorities, and can not be sustained upon principle.

First. As a question of authority, the elementary writers upon the subject generally concur that such a covenant cannot be made to run with the estate in the lands which the grantor of the rent charge held at the time. Platt on Covenants, pp. 65, 475; Rawle on Covenants for Title, chap. 8, p. 341; Burton on Real Prop , § 1102; 1 Smith's Leading Cases, notes to Spencer's case, p. 129 et seq., 4th Am. Ed.

Such has been the doctrine of the reported cases, so far as an expression upon the question has been elicited. *Brewster v. Kidgell*, Modern 170; *Randall v. Rigby*, 4 Mees & Wel., 130; *Ingersoll v. Sergeant*, I Wharton, 337.

It is true there is no reported case where such a point seems to have been distinctly made and passed upon, except *Ingersoll v. Sergeant*, 1 Wharton, 337; and in that case the decision was made to turn upon the point that the rent was a *reni-service* and not a *rent-charge;* and that there was a difference between the two as to attaching to the lands as a burden.

No elementary writer seems to have thought otherwise unless Sugden's work on vendors and purchasers be an exception. He cites but one case which he claims to hold the contrary, namely, *Holmes v. Buckley*, 1 Eq. Ca. Ab., 27, See 2 Sugden, 486.

That was a case where the owners of land granted a water course through it to a man and his heirs, and covenanted for themselves, their heirs and assigns, to cleanse it, and the covenant was held to bind the land in the hands of an assignee.

This case is like *Morse* v. *Aldrich*, 19 Pick., 449, and can be sustained on the same principle. There was a grant or contract for the possession of the lands for a specified purpose, which created a privity of estate between grantor and grantee, the reversion remaining in the grantor. It bears no analogy to a case brought upon the covenant to pay a *rent-charge.*

He cites *Roach* v. *Wadham*, 6 East, 289, where the defendant succeeded on another ground; and where this point might have been raised but was not, and after criticising some of the authorities which held against him he concludes as follows:

"Upon the whole it is submitted that covenants like those in *Brewster* v. *Kidgell* ought to be held to run in both directions; with the rent or interest carved out of or charged upon it in the hands of the assignee, so as to enable him to sue upon them: with the land itself in the hands of the assignee, so as to render him liable to be sued upon it," see p. 492.

This is all there is of athority in favor of such a doctrine; and the author does not pretend to find such a rule, but merely expresses his own view, that it ought to be so.

Second. As a question of principle, the doctrine that a covenant to pay a rent-charge attached to the estate in the lands as a service or burden by which that estate was afterwards to be held by subsequent assignees, can not be sustained.

Such a contract bears no resemblance to a contract which grants the right of possession and reserves a rent as the return or compensation for the possession. A rent-charge is an annuity granted by the tenant of an estate with a contract provision to enter upon the lands and make the amount by taking personal or chattel property. It is an incorporal hereditament in gross; that is, neither appendant nor appurtenant to the lands. Williams on Real Property. pp. 265, 273; *Van Rensselaer* v. *Chadwick*. 22 N. Y., 32. As there is nothing in its nature or character which can change the covenant from a personal one to affect the estate of the covenantor, the real question is whether the tenant of an estate in lands can add further obligations to the contract under which his tenancy is held. so that subsequent holders of the same estate shall be personally liable to fulfill such additional obligations as a service or condition incident to the estate. In other words the question is whether one party to a contract can change its obligations without consulting the other, and merely by making another contract with a stranger.

This is a very different question from the one, whether the covenant to pay a rent-charge runs or passes with it to the grantee of the rent-charge so that he can sue the covenantor. Upon that question there is a conflict of the authorities, 19 N. Y., 78, 81.

. That it may have been charged upon the lands creates no personal liability upon the purchaser.

A charge by devise creates no personal liability, *Deeks* v. *Strutt,* 5t`: Term Rep., 690; *Griffin* v. *Shonnard,* 18 John., 428; *Kelsey* v. *Western,* 2 Coms., 507.

Nor does a charge upon lands by a mortgage impose a personal liability upon the subsequent purchaser of the estate, *Stebbins* v. *Hall,* 29 Barb., 533; *Belmont* v. *Comun,* 22 N. Y., 439.

That payments may have been made does not create a liability to continue to pay. *Child* v. *Chappell,* 5 Selden, 257.

Nor does it work an estoppel upon the defendant that he shall not deny his liability, or insist upon his actual rights, *Lounsbury* v. *Depew,* 28 Barb., 48; *Phelps* v. *Phelps,* id., 152

IX. But this case does not depend alone upon common law rules. The covenant was made by a purchaser in 1789 of the estate in fee. Section 1 of the statute concerning tenures, was then in force, and expressly provided that the purchaser should hold the estate by the same services and customs by which the vendor had before held. 1 R. L., 70. The purchaser was not restricted from binding himself personally by that statute, but his personal obligations could not attach to the fee as a service or burden to be thereafter incident to the estate.

There was no room for doubt as to the meaning and intention of the statute. It was substantially a copy of the English statute of 1290, which has been ever since in force in England. It has never yet been denied but that the English statute was effectual to prevent the covenants of a purchaser of an estate in fee from attaching as a burden to the estate purchased. The criticisms of Sugden in regard to a rent-charge did not include such a case.

X. The plaintiff did not become the owner of the covenant upon which the action is brought by the will of his father.

First. The testator devised such estate or interest as he held in lands, and such rents only as were incident to such estate or interest. Such is the obvious meaning of the language of the devise relied upon.

Second. The testator, at his death, was not the owner of the lands in question, nor of any estate or interest therein. The allegation of the complaint, (fols. 6. 17 and 18), the evidence and the finding of the court,(fols. 44, 46), are conclusive as to this fact. As a question of law, the effect of the deed of the testator to Geo. Read is settled as leaving no estate in land in the grantor. 2 Selden, 467, and 19 N. Y., 68.

Third. The testator, at the time of his decease, was the owner of the rent and the covenant to pay it. But this was not an estate in the land, but a mere chose in action (2 Selden, 506; 19 N. Y., 91).

It was an incorporeal hereditament in gross; neither appendant nor appurtenant to the lands (Williams on Real Prop. ch. 4, p. 265, 273) and could not therefore pass under a devise of the lands. Had the testator intended to pass the property in any rents except those which were attached to lands owned by him, he would have so expressed his intention. The devise specifies rents incident to the lands belonging to the testator, and names no other. The fair inference is that he meant no other. The legal construction results in the same conclusion. *Herrington v. Budd*, 5 Denio. 321. *Payne v. Beale*, 4 Denio, 412.

Fourth. But supposing the rent charge passed by this devise, the covenant to pay it did not, directly. It could not pass except as an incident to the rent charge There may have been a disputed question in England, but is settled here that the covenant did not pass as an incident ; in other words, did not run with the rent-charge. 19 N. Y., 78, 81.

XI. The statute of 1805, and its reёnactments were held not to pass the covenants. or make them run with the rent, but to give the right and remedy which belonged to the covenantee. But when this action was commenced. that statute did not apply, nor did its reёnactments, by reason of the act of 1860, before cited.

The act of 1860 was not unconstitutional. because it did not divest the plaintiff of any vested right, but merely withheld a right which had been given by statute.

The statute of 1805, as reёnacted, will be found 1 R. S., p. 747 (5th ed., 3 R. S., 37).

Without that statute, the plaintiff could not bring an action upon the covenant, because the covenant did not pass as an incident. The statute did not give him the covenant, but only the same remedies by action as the testator had. This statute bears no analogy to the provisions of the Code requiring every action to be brought in the name of the real party in interest. The Code cannot aid the action, because it gives neither rights nor remedies; and without the aid of the act of 1805. the plaintiff had neither right nor remedy upon the covenant.

The statute of 1860 took away all that was given by the act of 1805.

This is a different question from the one in regard to the liability of the defendant as created by the one statute, or as taken away by the other, but the authorities cited to the second proposition of the seventh point, fully sustain this point.

A. BINGHAM,
Of Counsel.

In the Court of Appeals.

STEPHEN VAN RENSSELAER, *Respondent, agt.* ALBERT SLINGERLAND, *Appellant.*

Points for Appellant; Statement of the Case.

This was an action of ejectment, commenced in 1856—tried in September, 1860—and judgment for plaintiff, to which exceptions were taken by the defendant.

The facts relied upon by defendant, were that on the 9th of June, 1790, S. Van Rensselaer, deceased, was the owner in fee of the premises in question, and on that day sold and conveyed the same to Gerrit Seager, the purchaser agreeing to pay 15 bushels of wheat, 4 fat hens,

and to perform one day's service with carriage and horses, yearly, in
consideration of the sale and conveyance ; and further agreeing, that
if he failed in fulfilling his agreement, the grantor might enter and
distrain, and for want of distress, might reënter and have the premises again; that defendant became the owner in fee of the same estate
in 1847, and remained such owner up to the commencement of the
action, and in the meantime failed to deliver the wheat and hens and
perform the services according to Seager's agreement; that plaintiff
served a 15 days' notice, and more than fifteen days thereafter commenced his action.

A motion for non-suit was made and denied. The grounds of tho
motion were:

1st. That the deed to Seager was an assignment.

2d. That plaintiff had failed to prove an estate or interest in
the premises.

3d. That the condition of reëntry never came to the plaintiff, and

4th. That chapter 98 of the laws of 1805, did not apply to the case.

Points.

The points in the case of *Van Rensselaer agt. Henry Bonesteel*, and
Van Rensselaer agt. John Read, are to be regarded as applying to this
case: and in addition thereto, the following:

1. The plaintiff failed to show that he had any estate or interest
in the premises, as required by statute in order to maintain his action.
2 R. S., p. 303, § 3.

In order to maintain ejectment, the plaintiff must be the owner of
some corporeal interest; something tangible, of which possession may
be delivered by the sheriff. Ejectment will not lie for an easement,
for a rent-charge, or for any other incorporeal hereditament. Adams
on Ejectment, p. 18. *Northern Turnpike Co. v. Smith*, 15 Barb., 354.
Rowan v. Kelsey, 18 Barb., 488.

In *Child v. Chappell*, 5 Selden, 252, the rule is stated as follows:
" That the claim of title, or of some interest in the premises, spoken
of in the statute, must be such a claim as that, if it were reduced to
possession or enjoyment, it would constitute an actual occupation of
the premises, so as to authorize ejectment to be brought on that
ground." The plaintiff only claims to own the rent-charge, the right
to the wheat and hens and service- Allow him to have had all the
possession and enjoyment of which they were capable, no one will
claim that it would constitute " an actual occupation of the premises,
so as to authorize ejectment " against him.

The defendant owned the estate in fee in the premises, and the reversion thereof was in the state (2 Selden, 467, and 19 N. Y., 68,
before cited). That was a corporeal hereditament. The interest of
the plaintiff was an incorporeal hereditament. And there is no rule
of law by which the owner of the one interest can be entitled to the
possession of the other confessedly not belonging to him.

Ejectment is the recovery without prejudice to the right of property. He who enters under it can only be possessed according to

right. If he has a freehold, he is a freeholder. If he has a chattel interest, he is in as a termor. If he has no title, he is in as a trespasser. *Jackson v. Dieffendorph*, 3 John., 268, 9.

II. The condition of reëntry can not supply the want of title.

First. It is no estate or interest in the lands. *De Peyster v. Michael*, 2 Selden, 479, 506. *Payne v. Beale*, 4 Denio, 412. *Nicoll v. The N. Y. & E. R. R.*, 2 Kernan, 121, 139.

Second. There must be a reversion to which the condition is attached and in favor of which it is to operate, and the plaintiff must own that reversion in order to maintain ejectment. There was no reversion in the grantor in the deed upon which this action was commenced.

This case must not be confounded with a qualified, base or determinable foe. Such a fee results from a new contract for the holding possession of lands, and is not the assignment of a preëxisting contract. The base fee is a new estate and leaves the reversion in the grantor. Such a condition is called a limitation, because upon the happening of the contingency, the estate becomes *ipso facto* terminated. Taylor's Lan. & Ten., §§ 272, 273.

Third. The instrument upon which this action was brought, operated as the assignment of the entire estate held by the grantor; in other words, as the assignment of the contract under which the grantor held the prëmses, and of which the state was the party of the first part. A condition of reëntry in such a deed is inoperative upon the estate or contract transferred. The tenant on assigning, cannot alter the terms of the contract under which he holds. All the elementary rules as to conditions subsequent are in the way of it, as well as the general principle of our real estate system.

The elementary rules referred to are as follows:

1. A condition must be created and annexed to the estate at the time of making it, not at any time after. 2 Cruise Dig., p. 3, § 10. Shep. Touch., 126. 1 Bacon Ab., Conditions C. and E. 2 Bl. Com., 351. Taylor's Lan. and Ten., § 280.

The contract which gives the right of possession, in other words the lease, is the contract which creates an estate. An assignment of such a contract does not create an estate, and, therefore, a condition of re-entry would be inoperative.

2. A condition can not be made by, nor reserved to a stranger; but it must be made by, and reserved to him, that doth make the estate, and it can not be granted over to another, except it be to and with the land or thing unto which it is annexed and incident, Shep. Touch., p. 117; 1 Bacon's Ab., Conditions E; 2 Cruise Dig., p. 4, Title 13, Ch. 1, § 15.

3. A condition of re-entry can operate only by putting an end to an estate. A *condition* is a qualification annexed to an estate by the grantor, whereby the estate may be enlarged, defeated or created, upon an uncertain event. Taylor's Lan. and Ten., § 271; 2 Bl. Com., p. 151; 4 Kent, 123; Shep. Touch., p. 177, Ch. 6.

It can not be reasonably contended that a tenant, by an assignment of his tenancy, can annex conditions to the estate either to enlarge or defeat the estate; and on assigning he becomes a stranger to the premises and can not be benefited by a condition of re-entry.

III, The party who has no reversion can not maintain ejectment upon a condition of re-entry, *Doe* v. *Adams*, 2 Crompt. & J., 232 ; *Same* v. *Barber*, id., 674 ; *Same* v. *Lawrence*, 4 Taunt., 23 ; *Smith* v. *Parkhurst*, 3 Atkins, 139; *Scott* v. *Lunt's Adms.*, 7 Peters, 606.

The reason is obvious. It is no part of the functions of a condition of re-entry to transfer title from one to another. It can be used only to obtain possession in favor of a party who has the title ; and it operates only by putting an end to an existing estate, so that the owner of the reversion, the next preceding title or es'ate, may thus acquire the right of immediate possession. For that reason a condition can not be made to a stranger. The title to an estate can not be transferred from one to another, except by a deed in writing, 2 R. S., 134, § 6.

If the vendor has actually made a conveyance, his title is extinguished in law as well as equity, and it will not be pretended that he can maintain ejectment, *Blight* v. *Rochester*, 7 Wheaton, 548, 9.

The title of the vendee, though derivative, is adverse to that of the vendor. He enters and holds possession neither of nor for the vendor, *The Society, &c.*, v. *Town of Pawlet*, 4 Peters, 506, 7.

The same doctrine was held in *Boone* v. *Chiles*, 10 Peters, 224 ; and *Watkins* v. *Holman*, 16 Peters, 54.

This doctrine has been recognized in the recent cases in this state, which have held that the statute of 1805, and its re-enactments, made a rent-charge into a reversion or its equivalent, and thus introduced the relations of landlord and tenant, where they did not exist by the contract of the parties.

But there is no principle of the common law, whereby the right of property can be acquired by one individual from another by forfeiture.

IV. The relations of landlord and tenant did not exist between the parties to this action. They can be created only by a lease; and never by the assignment of a lease. The reservation of a rent or condition of re-entry, can not change an assignment to a lease, 2 Bl. Com., 317; 1 Platt on Leases, p. 19; Taylor's Landlord and Ten., §§ 16, 426, 431.

The recent decisions do not deny this doctrine, and hence the statute of 1805 is made to create the relations by retroacting upon the deed of assignment.

In that way alone can this judgment be sustained under our statute (2 R. S., 505, § 30). That statute is expressly limited to landlord and tenant.

V. The plaintiff was not the grantee or owner of the condition of re-entry. It did not pass by the devise of his father to him (*Van Rensselaer* v. *Ball*, 19 N. Y., 104). Conditions subsequent can only be reserved for the benefit of the grantor and his heirs ; and no other person can take advantage of a breach, *Nicol* v. *The N. Y. & E. R. R. Co.*, 2 Kernan, 121; *Payne* v. *Beal*, 4 Denio, 405; *Herrington* v. *Budd*, 5 Denio, 321.

Neither the English Statute, 32 Hen. VIII. ch. 34, nor ours of the same character, made such a condition either assignable or devisable. They merely provided that grantees of reversions might " have the same remedies by entry, action or otherwise," as the grantor or lessor might have had " if such reversion had remained in such lessor or grantor," *Hunt* v. *Bishop*, 20 Eng. Law & Eq., p. 542; and *Same* v. *Remnant*, 24 id,. p. 545.

In *Van Rensselaer* v. *Ball*, 19 N. Y., 104, the statute of 1805 was held to be indispensable to the action; that without the act the plaintiff was disabled from maintaining it.

In this case, before the judgment was rendered, the act of 1805, with all its re-enactments, was made inapplicable. The plaintiff was therefore disabled from maintaining the action. His case was brought within 2 Kernan, 121, before cited.

The latter act was not unconstitutional, because it did not divest the plaintiff of any thing. It merely withheld the remedy which the statute of 1805 had been construed to give him. There was no saving clause in the act of 1860, and the legislature of 1860 certainly had as much authority to withhold the remedy as the legislature of 1805 had to give it upon a pre-existing contract.

See authorities cited in the case of *Van Rensselaer* v. *Read* upon a similar point.

VI. The condition of re-entry was in violation of the statute concerning tenures in force when this indenture was made in 1790, and was therefore void (1 R. S., p. 70). It was an attempt to impose new services and new obligations upon the estate transferred under penalty of forfeiture. This was expressly forbidden by the statute. The condition was not only in violation of the letter of the statute, but of its policy and intention (see point IX in *Van Rensselaer* v. *Read*).

A contract prohibited by statute, either expressly, or by implication, will not be enforced by the courts, although the statute does not in express terms declare such contract void. *Barton* v. *Port Jackson Pl. R. Co.*, 17 Barb., 397; *Seneca County Bank* v. *Lamb*, 26 Barb., 595, 601.

A. BINGHAM.
Of Counsel.

In the Court cf Appeals.

STEPHEN VAN RENSSELAER, *Plaintiff, Respondent, agt.* HENRY BONE-STEEL, *Defendant, Appellant.*

Points for Plaintiff—FACTS.

This action was commenced on the 28th of April, 1855, to recover rent under a lease in fee, by indenture dated February 13, 1794. The complaint (fol. 6 to 25), the demurrer (fol. 33 to 36), the judgment entered thereon October 19, 1858 (fol. 53), and the appeal to this court on the 26th April, 1860 (fol. 57), present all the facts and questions in the case.

First Point. Every question raised by the demurrer and involved in the judgment, has been fully decided by the court of appeals in several cases, and particularly in the case of *Church v. Heidon*, decided on a similar demurrer, in October term, 1860, after the law of 1860 was passed.

Second Point. The law of April 14, 1860 (chap. 396), enacting that the law of April 9, 1805 (chap. 98), and its reënactments in R. L. and 1 R. S., 747, § 25, shall not apply to deeds of conveyance in fee, made before April 9, 1805, &c., can not affect or destroy the plaintiff's judgment, nor the rights upon which the judgment is founded.

1. The judgment appealed from was entered nearly two years before the law of 1860 was passed. This question, therefore, had no existence, and was not raised or "actually determined" in the Supreme Court, and cannot be considered on appeal in this court of review. *Magie v. Baker*, 4 Kernan, 434.

2. The rights of the parties having been "carried into judgment," ceased to be executory, "and stood independently of any statute," when the law of 1860 was passed. The *judgment* cannot be destroyed even if the statute had been necessary to sustain any of the proceedings thereto, and had been absolutely repealed. *Butler v. Palmer,* 1 Hill, 324, 333, 336; *Key v. Goodwin,* 4 Moore & Payno, 341, 345; *Palmer v. Couley,* 2 Comst., 182.

3. The plaintiff, whether he claims as devisee or assignee, or both, is entitled to the rent, and could, at common law, recover upon the covenants in his own name and legal right (*Scott v. Lint's* Adm'r, 7 Peters, 606, and other cases cited in 19 N. Y. R. 97, 99). At all events, "he could have prosecuted in the name of the grantor, or his heirs, for the benefit of the equitable owner." (19 N. Y. R. 85). If no legal remedies remained, he could recover in equity. (Story's Eq. Jur., 705, 712; 1 Paige, 90; 4 John. Ch., 287; 13 Price, 721; 2 Sch. & Le., 109; 1 Mer., 53; 8 Barr., 28). By the Code, §§ 69, 111, all distinction between legal and equitable remedies is abolished, and "the one civil action" which the plaintiff has brought, is the only form now permitted, and is sufficient to entitle him to recover upon any legal or equitable grounds. 19 N. Y. R., 85; 4 Selden, 119; 1 Grey's Mass. Rep., 327.

N. B. *For further points on the effect of the law of* 1860, *see the points (in Van R. v. Slingerland, herewith argued), which are annexed, and referred to without repetition.*

In the Court of Appeals.

STEPHEN VAN RENSSELAER, *Respondent, agt.* ALBERT SLINGERLAND, *Appellant.*

Points for Plaintiff, Respondent.—FACTS.

The judgment appealed from was for the recovery, for nonpayment of rent, of the lands granted by indenture, or lease in fee, dated July

9, 1790, between Stephen Van Rensselaer, grantor, and Gerrit Sager, grantee. (See fol. 60, refering to the complaint, for grant, fol. 31 to 33; for rent, fol. 33 to 34; for distress, fol. 36, 38; for condition for re-entry, fol. 39; 42, will of S. V. R., fol. 61, 62; default in payment of rent, fol. 63, 48; service of notice of intent to re-enter, fol. 49 to 51). The indenture, if necessary, can be read in full, as agreed (fol. 64) and a copy of similar indenture for another farm will be found in the case of *V. R. v. Petrie*, herewith argued. The plaintiff claims, as devisee of his father, S. V. R., the grantor, who died 29th January, 1839, (fol. 61, 62), and the defendant was the assignee of the estate of the grantee, G. Sager, by deed dated in January, 1847, (fol, 62), and was in possession when the notice of re-entry was served, (fol. 64, 49, 50), and when this action was commenced in August, 1856. The facts as found on trial, will be found stated as briefly as possible, fol 71 to 82.

First Point. The questions are all raised by the motion for non-suit, (fol. 65 to 68), and those upon the alleged grounds, numbered 1, 2, 3, 4, have been fully considered and decided by this court, *V. R. v. Ball*, 19 N. Y. R., 100; *V. R. v. Hays*, ib. 68; *V. R. v. Snyder*, 3 Kernan, 299.

The questions arising on the 5th and 6th alleged grounds have also been decided upon the law, as then existing, in the same cases above cited, which govern this case, unless the statute passed four years after this action was commenced, on the 14th April, 1860, (chap. 396), enacting that the law of April 9, 1805, (chap. 98), and its re-enactments in the R. Laws and R. S., (1 vol., 747, § 25), "shall not apply to deeds of conveyance in fee made before April 9, 1805," &c., affects and destroys the plaintiff's rights to the rents, and the remedy by re-entry given to assigns by the indenture.

As to that, the following points are made:

Second Point. Without the help of any statutes, and by force of the express words and agreement of the parties, the *assigns* are entitled to the rent, and all the remedies, including the re-entry, given to them by the indenture.

1. The *rent-charge*, as a hereditament, was always *devisable*, and *assignable* at law, and passed by grant, by either of the words, *rent, hereditament* or *tenement*, (Comyn's Dig. Title, Assignment A. Tit. Grant C. D. E. 1, E. 3. Tit. Estates by devise, L. and notes; 2 Roll., 57, 1. 15), and carried with it to the assignee the right to an action on the covenant, in his own name, *V. R. v. Hays*, 19 N. Y. R., 85, and cases cited.

2. By the express words of the indenture, (fol. 8 to 16), the *rent*, as the principal thing, and the incident, inseparable, remedial contract rights of *distress, action,* and *re-entry,* are all given, not only to the original party. S. V. R., but to his heirs and *assigns*, (*i. e.* the assignees of the *rent, Henningway* v. *Fernandes*, 13 Simons, 228), forever, and are assignable at common law, (*Scott* v. *Lunt's Admr's*, 7 Peters, 606; *V. R. v. Hays*, 19 N. Y., 86, 97, 98, 99, and cases there cited; *Main* v. *Green*, 32 Barb., 457, 458). In Comyn's Dig. Tit. Grant (C.), it is said that a right of common *sans nombre* in *fee*, could be granted over, and, Ibd. (D.), that a common *sans nombre* for *life*

3

or *years* could not. So, it seems of a *rent-charge*, for *Maunds'* case decides that the express words of the grantor make a *rent-charge* granted, *pro consilio,* &c., to A, and his assigns, for his *life,* and the incident right of distress, assignable, for in that respect, *modus et contentio rincunt legem,* (Coke's Rep., Pt. vii. p. 112). In feoffments *tenor est obserrandus; modus legem dat donationi,* (Wright's Ten., 151.)

3. If the contract was of such a nature that the parties did not fear vexation arising from assigns, they could agree that the rights should go to assigns, as well as they could give assigns the benefit of a warranty, or other covenant, or chose in action running with an estate. Many instances of such an effect of express contracts will be found, *V. R.* v. *Jewett,* 2 Coms., 147 ; Dormer's case, 5 Coke, 40, and ca. ci. The case put by Littleton, § 347, shows that *assigns* were not there mentioned, *Nichol* v. *N. Y. & E. R R.,* 2 Kernan, 121, and *Underhill* v. *Saratoga R. R.,* 20 Barb., 456, arose upon simple grants on *condition* that roads should be built, &c., without agreements as to right to re-enter by either the party or his *assigns.* In *V. R.* v. *Hays* the court found a declaratory statute, "which precisely met the case," and expressly reserve the question as to the common law right, p. 86.

4. The right to re-enter was therefore as much a *contract* right as the right to the rent ; both were *hereditaments,* and the common law interposed the same and all the objections to the assignment of the covenants for the payment of the rent as to the assignment of the right to re-enter, (19 N. Y. R., 103). If, therefore, the common law permitted the legal assignment of the principal or rent, and of the covenants, or permitted the covenants to be assignable in equity, giving the assignee the right to prosecute thereon, in the name of the grantor or his heirs, (19 N. Y. R., 85), there is no reason, and yet no authority, for saying that the incident remedy by re-entry, so expressly given to assigns, does not, at least in equity, go, like all securities, with the rent, to be enforced like the other remedies, (*Langdon* v. *Buel,* 9 Wend., 84). The right to enter for condition broken, may be enforced by the heir of the father, where the heir on the part of the mother is entitled to the land when recovered. Cruise Dig. Tit. Estate on condition, § 53.

5. The right of re-entry has become, under the relief afforded in equity, and now by statute practically a security for the rent. No absolute forfeiture could result immediately from a breach of the condition, nor from the actual entry and recovery of possession. 3 Denio, 337, 338 ; 2 R. S., 506, § 34, 36; Strange, 900; 2 Sellon's Pra., 127; 2 Salk., 297; 1 Paige, 414 ; 7 Paige, 352 ; 16 Vesey, 402 ; 18 Vesey, 56; 19 Vesey, 134; 2 Price, 200 ; 2 Mer., 459; 11 Met., 112.

Third Point. The plaintiff claims by devise, and could so take, without regard to the statute of 1805, because this right of re-enty was not a naked possibility, but was incident to, and coupled with, a valuable vested estate of fee simple in the *rent,* (2 Kernan, 132), and was *devisable* under the decisions, resulting in our State in the judicial conclusions, that before the R. S, "*descendible* and *devisable* were convertible terms," and that every possibility, except a naked possibility *not descendible to heirs. (Jackson* v. *Waldron,* 13 Wend., 222 ;

Bayard . Lawrence. 7 Paige, 76; Comyn's Dig. " Devise " III; *Jack-son* v. *Varick,* 7 Cowen, 239 and 2 Wend., 166; *Pond* v. *Bergh,* 10 Paige, 140).

Fourth Point. By the R. Statutes, the *rent*, and *condition* and right of re-entry, are *devisable*.

1. The grantor, S. V. R., if he had no technical *estate*, present, or expectant, in the *land*, had, at the common law, a present, vested, descendible, or fee simple estate, in the *rent*, and in the *condition*, and the right, on breach thereof, to re-enter and have the *land* again in fee.

2. These estates or rights were both inheritable, and therefore *hereditaments*. *V. R. v. Hays,* 19 N. Y., 77; *V. R. v. Ball,* ib., 100; *Jackson v. Topping,* 1 Wend., 388; *Hogeboom v. Hall,* 24 Wend., 146, 149; Cruise's Dig. Tit. Condition, 53; 3 Kent's Com., 402; 2 Bl. Com., 19, 20, 17, and n. 5 Wend's Ed. See also 1 R. S., 751, § 1 and p. 754, § 27, which make descendible real estate to include "every estate, interest and right legal and equitable in lands, tenements and *hereditaments*," except *leases for years*, &c., which, but for tde exception, would have gone by descent under the sweeping intent and words of the statute. For revisors' notes see 3 R. S., 2d Ed., p. 602. Then by 2 R. S., 57, § 2, it is declared that "every estate and interest in real property, descendible to heirs, may be devised."

This section, as the revisers say in their note (3 R. S., 2 Ed., p. 627), was "intended to comprehend every species of real property, and terminate the dispute then pending, whether all interests which descend to heirs can be devised." The dispute (11 Wend., 110), seems, from the opinions subsequently given in the Court of Errors (13 Wend., 178, 222), to have been considered as then already settled at common law, in accordance with the principles of the statute.

3. It has therefore been decided in *Hunter* v. *Hunter,* 17 Barb., 86 that a fee simple rent, and the incident conditional right of re-entry are devisable and assignable, and would pass by the words " *all my real estate in* ," etc., in a grant (p, 76), and by words " all my lands in," etc., in a will, where it was evident the testator thereby meant the rents, etc., and had no other lands located to satisfy the devise (p. 86, 87). *Payn v. Beal,* 4 Denio, 405, decides only: first, that such rents were not embraced in the terms used in the statute concerning sales on execution, because it was thought all the provisions of that act taken together showed only *property corporeal* was intended; and second, that if the statute authorized it, the rent had not in fact been sold properly (p. 413). The case of *Harrington v. Budd,* 5 Denio, 324, was decided upon the statute of wills of 1787 (p. 624), and presented only a question of construction on a devise of " my two hundred and fifty acres of land," etc., without anything to show an intent to pass rents, and where the testator had lands located as the will required.

Where the word *hereditaments* is used as it is in the devise in the present case (fol. 61), every thing passes which may be inherited, corporeal or incorporeal, real, personal and mixed. Coke Lit., 154, *a* ; Com. Dig. Grant E. 1; *V. R. v. Hays,* 19 N. Y., 77, case and exceptions, fol. 37; *V. R. v. Ball,* ib., 100.

The dicta of elementary writers, that the benefit of a condition is not *devisable* (2 Preston on Ab., 264), will not be found supported by the authorities cited, and would apply only to naked conditions, and not to rights of entry granted to assigns, and incident to a rent.

Fifth Point. The R. Statutes also declare this rent and condition, and right of re-entry, *alienable.*

1. " Every person capable of holding lands, (except idiots, persons of unsound mind and infants), seized of, or entitled to, any estate or interest in lands, may alien such estate or interest at his pleasure, with the effect, and subject to the restrictions and regulations provided by law." (1 R. S, 719, § 10). " And ' lands,' as used in this chapter, shall be construed as co-extensive in meaning with lands, tenements and *hereditaments.*" (Ibid p. 750, § 10).

There is no exception of any estate, or any class of hereditaments, from this power of alienation. The " effect " with which, and the " restrictions and regulations " under which the right is to be exercised, are " provided by law " in the various subsequent provisions of the statute concerning estates, trusts, deeds, etc., of which §§ 14, 16, 144, 147 afford examples.

2. To construe the clause, " subject to the restrictions, &c.," as limiting the intent and effect of the statute to the power as then existing, would take away all the effect from the statute, be inconsisten with its scope and purpose, and reduce it, in effect and substance, to the absurd declaration that any person could alienate anything which he could alienate.

3. In addition to the vested estate in the *hereditaments* alienable by that term of the statute, the owner thereof may fairly be said to be " *entitled to* " the *land,* conditionally before, and absolutely after breach; for " *title,*" in its strictest sense, " is where a man hath lawful cause of entry into lands, whereof another is seized, for which he can have no action, as title of condition." (Coke Lit., 345 *b,* 348 *a,* and in Thos. Ed., vol. 2, p. 127). That lawful *cause of entry* may be the right remaining after disseisin, or arising from a breach of condition, or, as in the present case, a right expressly granted and given by deed.

4. Section 35 (p. 725, 1 R. S.), concerning expectant estates, only declares them " devisable and alienable *in the same manner* as *estates in possession,*" and was inserted to prevent the renewal, under the statute above quoted, of the old question whether expectant estates were devisable and alienable like estates in possession. The plaintiff's right or estate in the *hereditaments* is not expectant, but present and vested.

5. The Revised Statutes thus declared all hereditaments transferable by devise and alienation, but the old provisions concerning grantees of reversions, &c., were properly embraced in substance in sections 23, 24, 25,, pages 747, 748, because they still remained necessary to give to the assignees, when not named, the entry to take profits, &c., where that was given to the grantor, and the actions like *debt* or *assumpsit* which the grantor had by the law only, and to give actions by and against executors, in many cases for rents in arrear; and they embraced, in a condensed form, the provisions of several other statutes, and authorized distress (not given by the statutes 32d Henry, 8), by executors where they would not otherwise have had it.

1 R. L., 384, §§ 17, 18. Such reënactment was, therefore, proper, although it was not, by reason of the other general provisions necessary, if it had ever been, to make either of the hereditamens involved in this case legally assignable.

6. The Revised Statutes not only thus declared all rights which were of such a real nature as to be *hereditaments* assignable, but abrogated all objections or reasons against the assignability of any of them interposed by the law of maintenance, of which, "not a vestige remains in this State." (*Sedgwick v. Stanton.* 14 N. Y. R,, 289, 300, 301; *Field v. Mayor*, &c., 2 Seld., 179, 186, 253).

7. The right of alienation is an inherent, and the most valuable incident of *property or contract rights*, and is the general rule. *Shep. v. Touch.* 118 Perk, 707, 708; *Plow.* 308; *Meech v Stoner*, 5 Smith, 29). The exceptions which arose from feudal tenures, and the fear of maintenance, have been reduced, at least as to *hereditaments*, to the restrictions now found in our statutes. It is absurd and unjust to suppose that the Legislature has intended to deprive the owners of rents—the most extensive and valuable class of hereditaments—and no one else, of all power to recover, as well as all right to alienate and devise their property.

8. If the case of *Nicholl v. The N. Y. & Erie R. R.* in this court, aud the similar cases in the Supreme Court, should be held consistent with the above cited provisions of the statutes (which, from an examination of the opinions and printed arguments, do not appear to have been suggested or considered in any of those cases); they were all decided upon a very different right and condition, by which, the parties left the rights of heirs and assignees, and the persons who could reënter, to be fixed entirely by the law, and did not, as in our case, give the condition, with its right of reëntry to the assigns by express grant.

Sixth Point. If the statute enabling grantees of reversions, *rents*, &c., to have the remedies of their grantors was ever necessary as to any of the plaintiff's remedies, it is still in full force, and is applicable to leases in fee. 2 *Jones v. Varick*, 184; 1 R. S., 363; 1 R. S., 647, '8.

1, The law of 1805, chap. 98 (see its preamble), was only declaratory, and was passed "to remove all doubts respecting the *true construction* of the act concerning grantees of reversions," &c., and enacted, that that act "shall be *construed* to extend," &c. It was a legislative declaration that the court, in suggesting such doubts (*Devisees of V. R. v. Platner's Executors*), had not construed that act correctly. The act of 1805 is still unrepealed, and declares in what manner the former act, as to grantees. &c., also in full force, is to be construed. as to all leases in fee made between 1805 and 1860. The law of 1860 does not direct, nor require the court, to construe the act concerning grantees of reversions differently in regard to leases made in 1804 than those made in 1807; ncr to construe it now differently from the legislative construction given to it in 1805. *Main v Davis*, 32 Barb., 457, 458, and cases cited.

2. The cases of *V. R. Executors v. Platner's Executors*, 2d Johnson's Ca., 22, and *Devisees of V. R. v. Platner's Executors*, ib., 24,

suggested doubts concerning the construction of the statute concerning grantees, &c.; but even the last of these cases, "assuming it to have been correctly decided," (19 N. Y. R., 81), which, as to the doubt suggested, we can scarcely do in view of the law of 1805, was an action by devisees against *executors*, for rent accrued after the death of their testator, and is no authority that any statute is necessary to sustain the action of covenant or re-entry by assignees, entitled to the rent, against *assignees* liable therefor, in pursuance of the terms of the indenture, for rent accrued, while the parties claiming and charged, stood in the privity or relation provided for by the indenture. The case, at most, decides, as is respectfully submitted, that the "express covenant of the parties upon which the right of action was said to depend," (page 24,) made the "covenant descend with the land, and equally with the rent, and, therefore, *personal representatives* could not, after the death of the parties, and *for rents accruing after the death of both*, either maintain or he *subject to an action*." (p. 26). The defendants were the only personal representatives in that case, and the decision necessarily seems to be put on the ground that the defendants, as *executors*, were not *subject to an action;* and for the reason that the parties intended to, and by their agreement did, make the covenant and its obligation binding, after the death of both parties, only upon the party who, by reason of the profits and ownership of the land while the rent accrued ought, from time to time, to be liable; and that for such rents there was no statute to sustain actions between the representatives of former parties, who had died before the rent accrued, where one representative was a *devisee*, and the other a *personal* representative. The term *executors*, in the contract, is satisfied by making executors liable for rent in arrear at the death of their testator, as is expressly decided in *Quain's appeal*, (10 Harris Penn. R., 510, 511,) where it is held that such covenants concerning a *perpetual rent charge*, do not make a liability continuing *forever* upon the personalty and executors of the covenantor, because the parties intended it as a covenant running with the land, transmissible by the *death* of the parties, and as to subsequent rents, ceasing as a personal covenant.

Seventh Point. 1. The plaintiffs' rights had all been acquired by devise or assignments, made long before the act of 1860 was passed, and while the law of 1805, whether necessary or not for any purpose, was in full force. Such rights would not be destroyed, or affected, by an absolute repeal of the law of 1805, (*Palmer v. Conley*, 2 Coms., 182), much less by the *enacting* statute of 1860, which by words of only future import, (*Johnson v. Burrill*, 2 Hill, 239), enacts that the law of 1805 *shall* not apply, &c., and must be construed and applied by the well settled rule as to enacting statutes, that the provisions of a statute cannot have a retrospective effect unless declared to do so by express words or positive enactment; *Butler v. Palmer*, 1 Hill, 334; *Main v. Green*, 32 Barb., 457; *Dash v. Vankleek*, 7 John., 477; *Wood v. Oakley*, 11 Paige, 403; *Berley v. Rampacher*, 5 Duer., 183; *Palmer v. Conley*, 2 Coms., 182; *Bedford v. Shilling*, 4 Serg. & R., 401; *Duffield v. Smith*, 3 Serg. & R., 590, 599, 599; *Torrington v. Hargreaves*, 3 Moore and Pay, 143.

2. The right of re-entry had been exercised by commencement of the action before the act of 1860 was passed, *V. R.* v. *Ball*, 19 N. Y., 107.

Eighth Point. 1. Having thus acquired the rents and right of re-entry the plaintiff is entitled to enforce them, under the only form of remedy, the one civil action now given by the Code. *Main* v. *Davis*, 32 Barb., 468 and ca. ci.; *Trull* v. *Granger*, 4 Selden., 119.

Ninth Point. 2. The Legislature having abolished the remedy by distress provided for in the indenture, (*V. R.* v. *Snyder*, 3 Kernan, 300), the act of 1860, if effectual, as claimed by the appellants, to take away all other remedies from the plaintiff, is unconstitutional and void, because destructive of the contract. (*Morse* v. *Gould*, 1 Kernan, 287).

C. M. JENKINS,
Of Counsel.

In the Court of Appeals.

JAMES S. KNOWLSON, *Respondent*, agt. JACOB WHITE, *Appellant.*

Points for Appellant—Statement of Facts.

This action comes here upon the appeal of the defendant from the judgment of the General Term, affirming judgment of the Circuit. The trial was on demurrer to the complaint, that it did not state facts sufficient to constitute a cause of action.

The action was brought for the breach of the covenants of Benjamin Gifford, contained in a contract made by and between Stephen Van Rensselaer and Gifford, April 26, 1796. That contract was one of sale and assignment of lands by Van Rensselaer to Gifford, and a covenant to pay therefor by Gifford to Van Rensselaer.

The defendant was claimed to be liable on the ground that he subsequently became the vendee of the same estate in the same premises, which had been sold and conveyed by Van Rensselaer to Gifford.

Points.

1. Unless the covenant sued upon was one, when made, which runs with the land as a burden so as to bind the assignees of the covenantor, this judgment can not be sustained. The first thing to be done is to ascertain the rule as to covenants running with the land as a burden.

First. The covenant must be contained in, or be a part of, a grant or contract, which created or originated an estate or interest in lands.

There are two classes of *contracts executed*, used in the commerce of lands between individuals, namely, those which create estates or interests, and those which assign or transfer estates or interests before created. Blackstone classifies them as 1, original or primary, and 2. derivative or secondary. (2 Bl. Com., 309, 310). Every deed or contract of conveyance of lands, either creates an estate or interest, or assigns an estate or interest before created. To run with the land as a burden, the covenant must be embraced in a contract of the first class.

Covenants between lessor and lessee contained in the deed of lease may run with both the reversion on the one side and with the estate demised on the other. This is one of the familiar rules of the common law, which has never been questioned. 2 Platt on leases, page 401.

Second. But it is not enough to make a covenant run with the land, that it is contained in a lease, and made between lessor and lessee. Even in such a connection, "although the covenant be for him and his assigns, yet if the thing to be done be merely *collateral to the land,* and doth not touch or concern the thing demised in any sort, there the assignee shall not be charged." Second resolution of Spencer's Case. See 1 Smith's Leading Cases, page 23.

The principle which underlies this rule is obvious, and founded in the character of the rights which individuals may have in lands. There are two fundamental rules peculiar to real property:

(1.) The original and ultimate right of property in all the lands of the state is in the state. (1 R. S., 718, § 1, Constitution of 1840, art. 1, § 11.) Both the statute and the constitution were simply declaratory of that principle as a fixed and unalterable rule of the common law. Williams on Real Property, p. 16.

This is a right which "can never pass away from the people by grant or otherwise, because it is the original and ultimate ownership of the political sovereign, and not the title or estate of an individual." The Trinity Church Case, 22 N. Y., 47.

(2.) The second fundamental rule is that individuals can only hold estates in lands at most. That is they can have nothing but a right of possession. See Williams on Real Property, p. 16. Smith's Landlord and Tenant, p. 2.

And, "the only way that an individual can acquire a right in real estate, is by grant, or by an adverse possession of twenty years under claim of title, in which case the court presumes a grant." *Curtis v. Kesler,* 14 Barb., 521. *Post v. Pearsall,* 22 Wend., 444.

In other words, individual rights in lands rest upon a *contract executed* which bestows the right; and they can exist no longer than the obligations of that contract continue. It follows, as a matter of course, that whatever covenants or agreements are contained in such a contract, touching or concerning the estate or interest granted, are a part of that estate or interest, and can not be separated from it. An assignment of the estate or interest is nothing more than the assignment of the contract upon which it rests, and the assignee becomes a party to the contract. So long as he remains assignee of the contract, he is entitled to the benefits and subject to the burdens of the covenants and conditions therein contained, so far as they touch or concern the estate. A party in possession of lands, who denies that he is in by any contract, either with the state or with an individual, virtually admits himself to be a trespasser.

A lease is a contract executed which gives or grants the right of possession and prescribes the terms and conditions of that possession. There is a good reason why a party who comes to such right by assignment, should fulfill the terms and conditions imposed by the contract.

So far, there is no dispute about the rule as to when and what covenants run with the land; and there are few, if any, of the rules of
the common law, the r. ason or principle of which is more obvious.
Third.—As to grants of interests in lands which fall short of being
estates, and which contain covenants concerning the interest granted,
there has been some dispute whether in such cases the covenants ran
with the land. It has, however, been held that where some interest
in the land is granted and the estate is left in the grantor, and the
grant is made to a party as the owner of an estate in other lands, and
there is a covenant touching or concerning the interest granted, made
at the same time with the grant, such a covenant will run with the
land, so as to bind the assignee of the covenantor. This rule em-
braces grants of water privileges, right of way and other easements.
(*Holmer* v. *Buckley*, 1 Ab. Eq., 27,) is an early case of that kind; and
Morse v. *Aldrich*, (19 Pick., 454,) a modern case of the same character.
For an elaborate discussion of this subject, see also *Weyman's Ex'rs.*
v. *Ringold*, (1 Bradford's Rep., 54–5.)

We submit that the principle of the rule is the same in both cases.
This will appear evident when we consider what an easement is, and
how it is constituted.

An easement is " a privilege without profit, which the owner of a
neighboring tenement hath of another, existing in respect of their
several tenements, by which the *servient* owner is obliged to suffer or
not to do something on his own land for the advantage of the *dominant* owner. (Gale and Whateley's Law of Easements, p, 5.) The
chief requisites of an easement are : 1. It must be imposed upon corporeal real property. 2. It must confer no right to a participation in
the profits arising from such property. 3. It must be imposed for
the benefit of corporeal property ; and, 4. There must be two dis-
tinct tenements, the *dominant*, to which the right belongs, and the
servient, upon which the obligation rests. (2 Bouvier's Inst., 170–1,
Nos. 1601 and 1605. *Wolfe* v. *Frost*, 4 Sand. Ch. Rep., 89.)

In other words, to constitute an easement, there must be two different parcels of land belonging to different individuals respectively.
The grant of the easement becomes appurtenant to the two estates,
as a burden or servitude to the one and as a benefit to the other.

Such a right cannot stand alone, and does not reach to the dignity
of an estate, because it does not carry with it the exclusive right of
possession, but only the use of the lands for a limited purpose ; and
does not therefore create the relations of landlord and tenant. If it
be to a person who has no estate, or to one who has, but it is not
annexed to his estate; it is not an easement but a mere license.
2 Bouvier's Inst., 171. *Rathbone* v. *McConnell*, 21 N. Y., 469.

An easement, like an estate, always presupposes a grant. 14 Barb,,
521; 22 Wend., 444.

The chief difference between a grant which creates an estate and a
grant which creates an easement, is in the quality of the interest created ; the one being an exclusive right of possession and the other
not. Both are equally interests in lands and both depend equally
upon *contracts executed*, which bestow the right. And, it is equally
true as to both, that no one can make himself out to be the owner of

the right except by making out that he is the party of the second part to the contract which created and sustains the right, either as the grantee or the assignee of the grantee ; and as a party, there is good reason why he should fulfill the contract. Upon that principle, it was held in Morse v. Aldrich, 19 Pick., 454, that a similar privity exists between the grantor and grantee, where a grant is made of any subordinate interest in land, as where there is a grant of an estate. In either case, the residue of the estate, or the reversion, being left in the grantor, the estate or interest granted is held of him, or of his grantee of that reversion.

II. Covenants contained in the second class of conveyances, namely, in deeds of sale and assignment, do not run with the land as a burden.

First. As a question of authority, there is no reported case which has ever held that the covenant of an assignee to his assignor can run with the land as a burden upon the assignees of the covenantor, No elementary writer upon the subject has ever put forth such a rule; nor is there a reported case, where counsel have contended for such a doctrine. A contrary doctrine has been very generally assumed. See notes to Spencer's Case; 1 Smith's Leading Cases, p. 22, *et seq.*; Keppel v. Bailey, 2 Mylne & Keene, 517; Hurd v. Curtis, 19 Pick., 463; Weyman's Exrs. v. Ringold, 1 Bradford's Rep., 53, and authorities cited; Vyvyan v. Arthur, 1 Barn. & Cres., 410; Webb v. Russell, 3 Term Rep., 393, and authorities generally.

Second. As a question of principle, such a doctrine is absurd. A tenant, on assigning his tenancy, creates no estate and grants no right; he only transfers a preëxisting right. His assignee takes and holds under the same contract as the assignor before held. The assignor ceases to be the party of the second part to the grant or lease; and his assignee succeeds him as the party to that contract.

The assignor cannot change the terms or conditions under which the lands are held; nor can he impose new or additional terms under which the lands are to be thereafter held of himself, or of his heirs or assigns. To hold that he could, would subvert the whole system of real property. Those who own estates, but have tenants under them, would be dependant upon the favor of their tenants; for, should the tenant assign, he would give his landlord a new tenant: but he might, at the same time, place himself between the landlord and his tenant, practically, if not nominally, as an intermediate lord ; and every subsequent assignee could do the same, and so on, without limit, until the proprietor of the land would be practically so far removed from his tenant by the intermediate assignors, that he could not collect his rent, while the intermediate assignors would have thrown off all liabilities, either to the landlord or to the tenant, the moment they made their respective assignments. It is impossible to conceive of a doctrine more destructive of the rights of property, or more threatening to the foundations of society, than such an one would present.

III. The contract between Van Rensselaer and Gifford, containing the covenant sued upon, was an assignment. This must be regarded as a settled question. Indeed, it is not denied by the plaintiff, but it is so set forth in his complaint. But independent of the form of the contract, or of the intention of the parties, our statute concerning tenures, which was in force when the contract was made (1796), fixed it as an alienation or assignment. That statute was both an *enabling* and a *disabling* act. It *enabled* every tenant in fee to sell and assign his estate at pleasure. It *disabled* him from leasing in fee, and it *disabled* him from imposing rents and services upon the estate transferred. The ability to assign was attended with the proviso, that the purchaser should hold the lands or tenements of the same fee, and by the same services and customs by which the person making such alienation before held the same lands or tenements. 1 R. L., 70, § 1.

That section was but the re-enactment of the English act of 1290, known as the statute *quia emptores*. It did more than prohibit; it disabled a tenant in fee from leasing in fee.

The effect of the English statute is well stated in Williams on Real Property, page 95, as follows:

"The giver or seller of an estate in fee simple is then himself but a tenant, with liberty of putting another in his own place. He may have under him a tenant for years, or a tenant for life, or even a tenant in tail, but he cannot now, by any kind of conveyance, place under himself a tenant of an estate in fee simple. The statute of *quia emptores* now forbids any one from making himself the lord of such an estate; all he can do is to transfer his own tenancy; and the purchaser of an estate in fee simple must hold his estate of the same chief lord of the fee as the seller held before him."

The effect of the statute is stated substantially in the same way by Smith in his work upon Landlord and Tenant, pages 5 and 89; and all the writers upon the subject have taken the same view.

Our statute has received the same construction by this court, in both *De Peyster v. Michael* (2 Selden, 467), and *Van Rensselaer v. Hayes* (19 N. Y., 73).

In the first cited case, this court said of our statutes: "*They put an end to all feudal tenures between one citizen and another, and substituted in its place a tenure between each landholder and the people in their sovereign capacity.*" 2, Selden, 504-5.

In the other case it was declared that "*The law forbidding the creating of new tenants by means of subinfeudation was always the law of the colony, and that it was the law of this state, as well before as after the passage of our act concerning treasures in 1787.*" 19 N. Y., 74.

And again, in the same case: "*The effect of this important enactment was, that—henceforth no new tenure of lands which had already been granted by the sovereign could be created. Every subsequent alienation placed the feoffee in the same feudal relation which his feoffor before occupied; that is, he held of the same superior lord by the same services, and not of his feoffor.*"

In both cases this court expressly declared that our laws upon this subject, at least as they existed previous to 1805, were precisely like the laws of England. 2 Selden, 504-5; 19 N. Y., 76.

The case before the court then stands in this way. Van Rensselaer owned an estate in fee, and sold and transferred it to Gifford. The title of Van Rensselaer necessarily presupposed a grant from the state, of which he was the original grantee, or the assignee of the original party. This court must, therefore, regard it as a part of this case, that there was a contract executed, older than the one sued upon, of which the state was a party of the first part, and Van Rensselaer before his conveyance to Gifford, the party of the second part; and after his conveyance, that Gifford was the party of the second part thereto; and by a transfer from Gifford that the defendant succeeded Gifford in the contract with the state. In other words, Van Rensselaer, Gifford and the defendant have successively been the tenants of the state, of the same estate.

So far this court has already decided in the cases before cited. The defendant was never, therefore, a party to the contract sued upon, and cannot be held liable thereupon, without holding that the distinction between a lease and an assignment, which has been a marked feature of the common law from its very origin, is and was a fallacy; and without holding that the statute *quia emptores* was of no effect, notwithstanding it had been held otherwise for six hundred years; or else, that all those distinctions and effects were wiped out by the act of 1805.

This distinction between a lease and an assignment, has been not only recognized by the courts and by jurists generally, but legislatures and statesmen have founded some of their most important acts upon it. In the constitutional convention of 1846, a provision was made as to agricultural lands, that there should be no lease or grant reserving rent or service of any kind for a longer period than 12 years. Had the legal minds which gave direction to that convention supposed it possible that rent or service could be legally imposed between vendee and vendor, or assignee and assignor, on sale or assignment, it is reasonable to suppose that they would have enlarged the terms of that provision so as to embrace sales and assignments.

The point they were seeking to attain, was the freedom of agricultural lands from servitude of any kind. But notwithstanding the restriction they imposed against grants or leases, if this judgment can be lawfully sustained, that is, if such servitude can be just as effectually imposed in connection with deeds of sale and assignment, they grossly failed to reach the end they aimed at by the constitutional provision. The purchaser of lands might covenant to labor every day in the year, or make any other lawful covenant, and if such covenant attached to the lands and fell upon his assigns because they might be named, every foot of land in the state might, and, in time would, be covered with oppressive and degrading obligations which would be constantly increasing.

IV. But even supposing the distinction between a lease and an assignment open to question, as a general rule, there would still be no doubt in a case like this, coming as it does within our statute of tenures of 1787.

First. The statute not only made every conveyance of a fee by an individual, an assignment of the fee, notwithstanding the parties may have expressed the intention, by the language of the instrument, that it should be a lease, but it also expressly provided that the purchaser should hold " by the same services and customs" as his vendor before held the same lands or tenements. This language was clearly intended to *disable* the vendor from imposing new or additional services and customs to be incident to the holding. It was more than a *prohibition*, it was a *disability* to impose new services or conditions.

Second. The ultimate purpose of the statute *quia emptores*, was to prevent estates in fee from becoming burdened with rents and services or any other imposition. The evil which the statute was designed to remedy, was the accumulated imposition of such burdens upon the lands by successive leases in fee.

The system of subfeuds was carried to so great a length that it broke down of its own weight. All the parties connected with the lands suffered from excess of the burdens imposed over and above the annual productions of the land. 2 Bl. Com., 91.

They first tried the remedy of partial prohibition upon leases in fee. That failed. Then came the total disability provision of the statute *quia emptores.* This has been regarded and treated as a perfect remedy in England since its enactment in 1290. Its entire success as a remedy has never even been questioned.

Third. This court expressed the opinion in *Van Rensselaer v. Hays,* (19 N. Y., 73), that the statute *quia emptores,* was introduced into this state under the colonial government, and has ever been here contemporaneous with the common law; that the statute of *tenures* was only declaratory of the law as it before existed. 19 N. Y., 74.

It should therefore receive the same construction here as in England. The rule upon this subject was stated Ch. J. Marshall in *Cathcart v. Robinson,* (5 Peters, 280), as follows:

" The rule which has been uniformly observed by this court in construing statutes, is, to adopt the construction made by the courts of the country by whose legislature the statute was enacted. The received construction in England at the time they are admitted to operate in this country, indeed to the time of our separation from the British empire, may very properly be considered as accompanying the statutes themselves and forming an integral part of them.''

It would be somewhat unreasonable to presume that our legislature, in the declaratory act, intended differently from the English act, as they expressed no different intention in the language which they adopted.

Fourth. But aside from the fact that the legislature adopted the English statute without any material change, they gave further evidence of their intention, by the last section of the same act, which was new and original. By that section, they provided so that grants of an estate in fee made by the state were to be *allodial* and not *feudal*; and to be held discharged of all rents and services whatsoever. The intention of this section is plain. The state was thus prevented. not from making grants or leases in fee, but from attaching to such estates any rents or services as conditions or burdens upon the estates. By the first section, individuals were disabled from imposing burdens upon estates in fee, but this disability did not embrace the state. Hence the last section was provided in order to restrain the estate in that respect. There was nothing in either section to restrain the state or any individual from making leases for life or for years, and imposing thereupon rents and services. There was nothing to prevent the state from making grants in fee; she was only prevented from imposing rents and services to run with the land. She could take the personal obligation of the grantee and enforce it, but could not make that personal obligation a condition or burden upon the land.

It is apparent, therefore, from these two sections, that the policy of the legislature of 1787, was to preserve estates in fee, in all cases, free from the imposition of rents and services to grow due either to the state or to individuals. The first section secured against rents or services to be reserved to individuals, on estates in fee, and the last against rents or services to be reserved to the state upon granting lands in fee. Neither of these sections had any effect upon leases for life or years.

The four intermediate sections had no bearing upon either the first or the last section. They were simply re-enactments of the English act of 12 Charles II, ch. 24. Sections two and three abolished military tenures with all their incidents. Section four declared how military tenures should thereafter be regarded; and the fifth section saved rents and services certain, if any existed in connection with the military tenures abolished. Such rents and services were consistent with soccage tenure, and therefore they were to be saved.

The revisers expressed the opinion that no military tenures ever existed here; and that, consequently, those sections were unnecessary, and of course without effect. No one has ever questioned that opinion; and our laws have been declared to be similar to the laws of England upon this subject, at least before the act of 1805 2 *Selden*, 504-5 ; N. Y., 76, before cited.

V. It has been urged, by way of precedent or argument, that the courts of this state have always assumed that the assignees of the grantee were liable upon such covenants.

The answer to this is so apparent, that it is remarkable that such an argument was ever made by any one. So far as there have been such assumptions by the courts, or by the lawyers, they have followed from the ulterior assumptions that the statute *quia emptores* was not in force here; and that, consequently, the parties claiming rents were feudal lords, and the parties of whom they claimed, feudal or manor tenants, in the true and legal sense of those words. The one were assumed to be the proprietors or owners of the soil, and the other merely their tenants. With such ulterior assumptions at the foundation, the assumption that the covenants ran with the land, so as to fall as a burden upon the assigns of the covenantors, was a matter of course ; and such have been the ulterior assumptions in all the cases relied upon in that argument. See *Jackson* v. *Schultz*, 18 Johns, 179. *Watts* v. *Coffin*, 11 Johns, 495. *Lush* v. *Druse*, 4 Wend. 313. *Van Rensselaer* v. *Bradley*, 3 Denio, 135. *Van Rensselaer* v. *Jones*, 2 Barb. 643. *Van Rensselaer* v. *Gallup*, 5 Denio, 460.

Upon such assumptions alone, the class of interests which has sought distinction under the name feudal or manorial has been sustained, so far as it has received countenance from any source. Now when this court decided that the statute *quia emptores* was in force here and always had been in force, they pronounced those ulterior

assumptions to be false and unfounded. This destroyed the foundation of the cases relied upon as authority to make the covenants run
with the land. Those cases afford no authority for the inference that
it is immaterial whether the statute was or was not in force; whether
the instrument sued upon was a lease or an assignment; whether the
claimant of rent owned the land or not; whether the contestant was
the tenant in fee of the estate or of the claimant; and those cases are,
therefore, no authority in favor of this judgment, for it can not be
sustained, without holding all those points, to be immaterial.

As to the statute of 1805, and other points, apply the points presented to this court at the January term, 1863, in the case of *Van
Rensselaer* v. *Bonesteel.*   A. BINGHAM, of Counsel.

In the Court of Appeals.

JAMES S. KNOWLSON, *Respondent, agt.* JACOB WHITE, *Appellant.*

JAMES S. KNOWLSON. *Respondent, agt.* PETER A. ALLENDORPH, *Appellant.*

JAMES S. KNOWLSON, *Respondent, agt.* LEWIS ALLENDORPH, *Appellant.*

Points for Respondents.

These three cases all arise on demurrer to complaints in covenant
for rent on leases in fee made by the late Stephen Van Rensselaer.

The questions involved are precisely the same with those
presented in the case of *Van Rensselaer* v. *Bonesteel,* No. 46 on
the annual calendar, which was argued on the 15th of January, 1863.

That case being now pending, it is supposed that a new argument
will not be heard on the same questions, and the points then submitted in behalf of the respondent are referred to as equally applicable
to these appeals.   JOHN K. PORTER,
                         Counsel for Respondent.

In Court of Appeals.

STEPHEN VAN RENSSELAER *agt.* JOHN READ.

SELDEN, J. A brief statement of the principles which appear to be
definitely settled, touching the rights and liabilities of parties under
instruments of the nature of that which forms the foundation of the
present action, by enabling us to see distinctly what remains undetermined, will be of service in the examination of the questions now
presented for decision. The following may be regarded as principles
thus settled.

1. That since the passing of the act of 1787, "concerning tenures"
(however it may have been before that time) it has not been possible
to create any new tenures, in this State, upon conveyances in fee.
Such conveyances operate as *assignments* and not as *leases*, whatever
name maybe given to them, and leave neither any reversion or possibility of reverter in the grantor, (*De Peyster* v. *Michael,* 6 N. Y. 467;
Van Rensselaer v. *Hays,* 19 Id., 68).

2. That an annual rent, issuing out of the land reserved in such
conveyance, to the grantor, his heirs and assigns, forever, with a
covenant on the part of the grantee for its payment, together with a
right of distress and re-entery in case of non-payment, although not a

rent-service for want of a reversion in the grantor, is a fee farm-rent, or, if not strictly such (Bradly on Distress, 34; Harg n. 5, on Co. Little, 143, b. 19 N. Y., 76) it is a rent-charge in fee, and equivalent to such rent-charge granted by the owner of lands in fee, (Little, § 217; Co. Little, 143. b; Gilbert on Rents, 16, 17, 39; 2 John., cases 26; 2 Cow., 659; 13 N. Y. 299; 19 Id., 77, 78, 100.

3. That such rent is a hereditament and descends, in the absence of other disposition, to the heirs of the party to whom it is reserved, and is devisable and assignable in all respects like other incorporeal hereditaments, 2 Sanders on Uses and Trusts, 32, 5th ed., Lond., 1844; Shep. Touch., 238; Lade v. Baker, 2 Ventris, 149, 260, 266; Maunds' case, 7 Co., 286; 2 John. Cases 17, 24; 12 N. Y., 132; 19 Id., 68; Id., 100.

4. The right to distrain, and the right to maintain actions of annuity, and assize of novel disseisin, at common law, followed the ownership of the rent, when it passed from the person to whom it was reserved, whether it passed by descent or assignment, (Vechte v. Brown, 8 Paige, 212; Bradly on Distresses, 51, 52; Adams on Distresses, 36; Maunds' case, 7 Co., 28 b.; Co. Little, 144, b. and Harg, Note 1; Roscoe on Real Actions, 65; Gilbert on Rents, 83, 100; Little, §§ 233, 235.

Attornment by the tenant was necessary to entitle the assignee to distrain or to maintain annuity and actual seizen of the rent by payment of a part to authorize an action of assize; but that necessity, at least so far as related to attornment, was removed in England by the statute, 4 Anne, ch. 16, 59, which was early re-enacted in substance, and has since been kept in force in this State, (2 Sanders on Uses and Trusts, 40 to 46; Butler's Note, No. 272 to Co. Little, tit. 3, 309, b.; Gilbert on Rents, 32, 33, 51, 52; Doug., 624; Strange, 108; Yelv., 135; 2 Greenl. Stat., 115; 1 R. L., 525, § 25; 1 R. S. 739, § 146).

5. That the covenants entered into by the grantee of the lands in behalf of himself, his heirs and assigns, are covenants real, which run with the land, and are binding upon the heirs and assigns of the covenantor successively, as to all breaches of such covenants which occur during their respective ownership of the lands. *Van Rensselaer v. Hays,* 19 N. Y., 68; Platt on Covenants, 493, 494.

6. That a devise or assignment of the rent gives to the devisee or assignee at least the equitable interest in the rent and the right to equitable remedies for its recovery, without any aid from the act of 1805, partially repealed by the act, ch. 396, of the laws of 1860, (19 N. Y., 85, 86.)

7. That the personal representatives of the original grantor, to whom the rent was reserved, can maintain no action on the covenant, for the payment of rent, on account of any default in payment occurring after the death of such grantor, (*The Executors of Van Rensselaer* v. *The Executors of Platner,* 2 John. cases, 19.

8. That devisee or assignee of the rent, can maintain no action against the personal representatives of the original covenantor, on account of any default in payment of rent, occurring after the death of such covenantor, (*The Devisees of Van Rensselaer* v. *The Executors of Platner,* 2 John. cases, 24.

9. That the terms of the devise to the plaintiff are sufficient to vest in him the right to the rent in question.

Several cases have been decided by this court, in which the right of the present plaintiff, under the devise in question, to rents of the character of those here claimed, has been sustained, and although the subject of the sufficiency of the devise to vest the title to the rents in the devisee, does not appear to have been specially noticed by the court, it is hardly possible that it could have passed unobserved, and the decisions in those cases, if not conclusive, raise a strong presumption in the plaintiff's favor upon this point. (*Van Rensselaer v. Snyder*, 13 N. Y., 299; *The Same v. Hays*, 19. 25, 68; *The Same v. Ball*. Id. 100. But regarding the question as an open one. I entertain no doubt that the language of the devise is broad enough to embrace the rents.

In the case of *Hunter v. Hunter*, (17 Barb., 28. 86), such rents were held to pass by the words " all my lands in the county of Greene."

Whether perpetual rent charges are properly denominated lands or not, they certainly come within the terms, " lands, tenements, and hereditaments " used in the present devise. Lord Coke says (Co. Litt., b. a). " Tenements is a large word to pass not only lands and other inheritances which are holden, but also offices, *rents*, commons, profi's *apprender*, out of lands, and the like wherein a man hath any frank tenement and whereof he is seized, *ut de libero tenemento*. But hereditament is the largest word of all in that kind, for whatsoever may be inherited is a hereditament, be it corporeal or incorporeal real, personal or mixed," (2 Roll. Ab., 57; *Rich v. Sanders*, Styles, 261, 278) That rent-charges in perpetuity are hereditaments has never been questioned. (2 John., cases 21, 26; *Jemmott v. Cooley*, 1 Lev., 170; S. C., 1 Saund., 112).

From the foregoing statement, it will be seen that the reservation of the rent in question is valid; that the covenant for its payment is a covenant real, running with the land, binding the defendant personally for its payment, (his ownership of the lands, when it accrued being undisputed) and that the plaintiff, by virtue of the devise from his father, was the owner of the rent, when it became due, having at common law the right to distrain for it, or to maintain an action of annuity for its collection. The further question is now presented, whether the devisee or assignee of the rent, may either at common law, or by virtue of any statute now in force, maintain an action on the *covenants* for the rent against the grantor or assignee of the covenantor.

The *burden* of the covenant, as we have seen, runs with the land, against the person who is in equity bound to pay the rent; does the *benefi'* of such covenant run with the *rent*, in favor of the person who is in equity entitled to receive it? If the assignee o the rent cannot avail himself of the covenant for its payment, one object of the parties to the covenant will fail. They covenanted for acts to be performed by and to each others, heirs and assigns *annually forev r*, in regard to this land. These acts were designed to be performed *directly* between such heirs and assigns, without the necessity of maintaining the expensive and cumbrous machinery of perpetual personal

4

representatives ol the parties. The decisions which have been referred to, show that on the part of the person bound to pay the rent, no such machinery is necessary; that the law deals directly with him, as holding the land charged with the rent, and therefore in law as well as in equity, bound to pay it. That the legal and the equitable duties accompany each other, both following the title to the land into whatever hands it may go, the assignee taking the place of the covenantor, and being bound by his covenants so long as he remains such assignee, and no longer. (Platt on con., 496). The same decisions show, also, that on the other side the equitable right to receive the rent passes to the assignee in the same manner as the equitable obligation to pay it follows the title to the land. It is claimed on the part of the defendant that the legal right of action on the covenant does not pass with the rent to the assignee, but is either extinguished by the assignment, or remains in the original covenantee or his personal representatives. The case of *Hays*, ab ve cited, shows that the covenant is not extinguished by the assignments; and no adequate reason caň be given for d nying to the assignee of the rent the right to maintain an action upon it. The only reason which has been assigned, in the authorities to which we have been referred, for such denial is that upon which the commoň law prohibited the assignment of all choses in action the prevention of maintenance. But the covenant for the payment of rent is not within this rule.

It is not a covenant in gross or a mere chose in action, (*Stevenson v. Lambard*, 2 East, 576), but is a part of the security for the payment of the rent. The rent itself being assignable, the covenant for its payment should, it would seem, be assignable, to the same extent, for the reason given by ch., Baron Gilbert why a *nomine pœnæ*, when provided for in the lease, passes to the assignee of the rent, viz: " because whosoever has a right to the rent ought to have all that security for the payment of it which was taken on the original creation of it." (Giibert on Rents, 143, Cro. Eliz., 895, 7 Peters, 605, 6).

Rent *due* is a mere chose in action, and not assignable, but it is otherwise of rent not due (Bradley on Distresses, 52. Adams on Distresses, 36). The covenant for its payment should, therefore, be assignable before breach, but not after. It was so held in *Demarest vs. Willard*, (8 Cow., 206, see T. Raymond. 200.) Even if the law was clearly settled in England that such covenants were not assignable, I should be unwilling to follow that rule unless it had been already recognized by our courts, especially since we have abrogated the doctrine of maintenance, upon which alone it rested. It is, however, far from being settled in England, and no precedents in its support in this state have been brought to the notice of the court; on the contrary, there are several decisions leading to the opposite conclusion.

In the case of Hays the right of the assignee to maintain an action on the covenant for the payment of rent in a lease or indenture, like the present was sustained; but the decision was placed upon the effect of the act of 1805, which was held to extend to the assignees of rents reserved in conveyances in fee, the same remedies by action for the non-performance of covenants against the grantees and their assigns, which were secured to the assignees of reversion by ch. 7 of the laws of 1788.

Since that case was decided, and prior to the commencement of the present action, the legislature, by ch. 396 of the laws 1860, has declared that the act of 1805, and its reënactments, should not apply to deeds of conveyance in fee made before the 9th day of April, 1805. The plaintiff's cause of action was complete under the act of 1805, prior to the passing of the act of 1860, and the constitutionality of the latter act, as applied to the present action, is therefore denied. The act of 1805 has been held to affect the remedy only, and not the contract, and for that reason not liable to this objection, when urged by the assignees of the covenantor (19 N. Y., 68.) The objection to its repeal would nevertheless be effectual in favor of the plaintiff, if such repeal would deprive him of all substantial remedy for the recovery of the rent, but not otherwise. As I am satisfied that his remedy was not affected by the repeal, this question becomes immaterial.

It is insisted on the part of the plaintiff that the act of 1788, as reenacted in the Revised Statutes (vol. 1, p. 749, §§ 23, 24), without the declaratory act of 1805, (id. § 25), is broad enough to embrace the present case, and to give the assignee of the rent a right of action on the covenant for its payment. I think the act in its present form might fairly receive that construction, but its title as originally passed, viz: "An act to enable grantees of reversions to take advantage of the conditions to be performed by lessees, would create a doubt whether the general expressions contained in the act were not intended to be limited to grantees or assignees of reversions, though such limitation is not expressed. So far as the statute has received the attention of judges, the opinion appears to have been entertained that its benefits were confined to parties having the reversion of the lands to which the conditions or covenants related, and such is the established construction of the statute (32 Hen., 8) ch., 34, after which our statute was modelled. The solution of the present question, therefore, depends upon the common law, or upon recent statutes relating to the prosecution of actions. The first ground upon which the judgment in this case is sought to be sustained, without the aid of the acts of 1788 and 1805, is that the covenant for the payment of the rent, is not a merely personal covenant, but a covenant real, the benefits of which passed to the plaintiff on the devise of the rent to him. This question has been much discussed by judges and elementary writers, and cannot be regarded as entirely at rest on either side of the Atlantic. I shall not attempt to review the cases, as very little could be added to what appears in the English and American notes to Spencer's case (1. Smith's Leading Cases, 22), and in the recent treatise of Mr. Sugden on Vendors and Purchasers.

Mr. Sugden says (vol. 2, p. 482) "the rent-charge is an incorporeal hereditament, and issues out of the land, and the land is bound by it; the covenant therefore will run with the rent in the hands of an assignee; the nature of the subject, which savors of the reality, altogether distinguishes the case from a matter merely personal." Again, at page 492, after reviewing the English cases bearing upon

the question. he says "upon the whole, it is submitted that covenants
like those in *Brewster* v. *Kidgell*," which was the case of a rent-
charge in fee with a covenant for its payment, free from taxes, "ought
to be held to run in both directions, with the rent or interest carved
out or charged upon it" (the land) "in the hands of the assignee so
as to enable him to sue upon them, with the land itself in the hands
of the assignee. so as to render him liable to be sued upon it."

This conclusion is confirmed by the decision of the Supreme Court
of the United States, in the case of *Scott* v. *Lunt's. Administrators*,
(7 Peters., 596), in which the assignee of a rent-charge in fee, created
by an indenture in all material respects similar to that under which
the plaintiff claims, was entitled to maintain an action of covenant
for the rent, against the administrator of the covenantor. The difference of opinion on this question among judges and elementary writers
has, I think, mainly arisen from a misunderstanding by some of them
of the remarks of Lord Holt in the case of *Brewster* v. *Kidgell*, as
was shown in the opinion of Judge Denio, in the case of *Van Rensselaer* v. *Hays*, (supra). In that opinion the learned judge, after referring to the passages above quoted from the treatise of Mr. Sugden,
says, "the great learning of the author, afterwards as Lord Leonards,
Lord Chancellor of England. would incline me to adopt his conclusions, were it not that we have a precedent the other way in this
State." referring to the case of *The Devisees of Van Rensselaer* v.
The Executors of Platner. (2 John. Cases, 26). I do not understand
the decision in that case as in conflict with the opinion of Mr. Sugden,
on the contrary, when considered in connection with the case of *The
Executors of Van Rensselaer* v. *The Executors of Platner*, decided at
the same time, it appears to me very strongly to confirm that
opinion.

Both those actions were brought to enforce the covenants for the
payment of rent, entered into by Platner. the defendant's testator, in
an indenture executed in 1774, by which John Van Rensselaer conveyed to him in fee simple. reserving rent, and rights of distress and
re-entry, and with covenants for payment on the part of the grantee,
in all respects similar to those contained in the indenture on which
the plaintiff relies in the present action.   In the case in which *The
Executors of Van Rensselaer* were plaintiffs, they had claimed in their
declaration, for several years' rent, which accrued during the life of
their testator, and for one year's rent which became due after his
death, and had obtained a verdict for the whole. All the rent had
accrued after the death of Platner, the original covenantor. A motion
was made in arrest of judgment. and two grounds were relied upon in
support of the motion.   *First*, that the executors of Platner were not
liable for rent which accrued subsequent to the death of their testator.
Second, that the executors of Van Rensselaer, could not recover for
rent which accrued subsequent to the death of *their* testator.   It was
held that the executors of Platner were liable on the express covenant
of their testator, notwithstanding the descent of the land to his heirs.
and that the recovery so far as it embraced rent which became due
during the life of the plaintiff's testator was correct; but that the
plaintiff had no right of action. for the year's rent which became due

after the death of their testator, and for that reason judgment was arrested. Kent, J., said, " it is clear that the executor can only go for rent due and payable at his testator's death *where the rent as in the present case goes, on the testator's death, to his heirs.*"

In the other case parties to whom John Van Rensselaer had devised the rent, were plaintiffs and had obtained a verdict against the executors of Platner, for rents which became due subsequent to the death of both Platner and Van Rensselaer. The judgment was arrested, not on the ground that the devisees were not entitled to maintain an action on the covenant, but on the ground, that the defendants were not liable t- theplaintiffs' *deviseer* for the rent, "which," as the court says, " is created by reason of the contract, and is by reason of the profits of the land, wherein none is longer chargeable with them, than the *privity of estate continues with them.*" It was held that the *the executors of* the covenantor were liable only by force of the personal contract of their testator, without reference to the land, and in that respect were liable only to those " legally competent to represent the *mere personal rights*" of the covenantee, which the plaintiffs clearly were not. Ch. J. Lansing, who delivered the opinion of the court said, " this rent is a fee farm-rent.'

Harg. Co. Little, 145 b. n. 5. *on rent-charge*: it is perpetual. The rent is real estate, and so, certainly, is the estate out of which it issues. The rent and the land granted are equally transmissible to the heirs of the person seized. * * * If the *covenant descends with the land, it must equally descends with the rent isuing out of the land,* and if so, the personal representatives can not, after the death of the parties, and for rents accruing after the death of both, *either maintain or be subject to an action* on the privity of contract, the defendants cannot be liable to the plaintiffs, because they are not legally competent to represent the mere personal rights of the testator, arising from the contract, they cannot otherwise represent him, than as the rights of the testator devolve upon them; but those being merely taken as devisees, they are strictly confined to the real estate. If they claim against the defendants deducing their title by the devise, they must claim on the principle that the common ligament, *the estate charged,* unites them in interest, as privies, with the defendants; but it is not pretended that the executors hold the estate, or have any interest in it, and on this ground the action is not attempted to be maintained." All which this case decides, therefore, is that the executors of a person who covenants to pay a perpetual rent-charge are not liable on the covenant to any person except the covenantee and his personal representatives, and in connection with the previous case, which decides that such personal representatives cannot recover for rent falling due after the death of their testator or intestate for the reason that the rents go to the heirs or devisee, it shows that the *executors* of the covenantor can never be made liable for any default which does not occur during the life of one of the original parties to the covenant. Possibly this limitation of the liability of covenantors, may not be consistent with the common law rules, as recognized in England, (Platt on Cov., 194, 195; Id., 493; 7 Peters, 604,) but it is in substantial accordance with the manifest intention of the parties, as expressed in the contract, and as strongly recommended by its justice and convenience. These cases having been decided by a court of great learning and ability more than fifty years since and the correctness of the decisions, so far as I am informed, never having been questioned, I cannot do otherwise than to recognize them as expressing the proper limitation of liability of parties in covenants for the payments of perpetual rents. The Supreme Court of Pennsylvania has decided that the liability of the personal representatives of the covenantor in such a case extends only to defaults which occur during the life of such covenantors. Lawrence, J., in delivering the opinion of the court, among other things, says " the grantor of the land cannot be presumed to have placed any value on such a covenant ; for the personal covenant of the original grantee is as nothing in a series of tenants lasting forever. The real security is the covenant running with the land and encumbering it ; and this is the essential reliance of the owner of the rent. * * * It is a covenant, payable in contemplation of the parties, out of the profits of the land, and it would be entirely unreasonable that the law should hold the administrator for the rent, when it gives the land to the heir (Quains' Appeal, 22; Penn. State Rep., 10 Harris, 510). The obligation of the covenant, therefore, which passes from the original covenantor to his grantee of the land and the other grantees in succession, (Platt on Covenants, 480, 487), binding them to pay the rent accruing during their ownership, cannot, when the rent has been assigned, be enforced, either by the personal representatives, or by the heir of the covenantee, for want of any privity either of contract or estate between them and the assignee of the land, and such covenant becomes entirely nugatory unless it can be enforced by the assignee of the rent. I am satisfied that it is not extinguished, but may be enforced by the assignee of the rent, that there is such a privity of estate between the assignee of the rent, who is entitled to demand and receive it, and the owner and occupant of the land, by the covenant who is bound to pay it; as entitles the former to maintain an action upon the covenant for its collection.

But two reasons have been assigned why the benefits of the covenant to pay the rent does not run with the rent in the same manner as its burden runs with the land. One is, that covenants do not run with land, except where *tenure* exists, and the other, that covenants can only run with *land*, and that rents are not land. Neither of these positions is sound. It has often been held that covenants, both as to their benefits and their burdens run with land, where no tenure in its strict sense exists between the parties. The case of the Prior of the Convent, who, with the assent of his convent, covenanted with the Lord of a Manor to celebrate divine service, for the lord and his servants, in his chapel, parcel of the manor, is a case of this kind. The covenant was held to pass to the grantee of the manor, although there was nothing in the shape of tenure between the parties (5 co. 17. b. In the case of *Brewster vs. Kedgell*, before referred to, a covenant to pay a rent charge in fee free from any deduction for taxes, was held to run with the land, without the aid of tenure.

In *Holmer* v. *Buckley*, (Prac. in Ch. 39 ; 1 Eq. Cas. Abr. 27. fol. 1.) one had granted, in 1622, a water-course through his lands and covenanted to cleanse it; and in 1691, after the lands and water course had passed through several assignments, it was held that the covenant was binding in favor of the assignee of the water course against the assignee of the land.

The case of *Morse* v. *Aldrich*, (19 Pick. 425,) was of a similar character. There had been a grant of a right to dig and carry away mud from the mill pond of the grantor, with a covenant on his part that he would draw off his pond when requested in August or September, not exceeding six days in each year, to give an opportunity to dig and remove the mud. The action was against a portion of the heirs and the assignees of the other heirs, of the covenantor, for a breach of the covenant. The court held the defendants liable on the ground that the contract was a grant of a subordinate interest in the lands, and the reversion or residue of the estate being reserved by the grantor, all covenants in support of the grantor in relation to the beneficial enjoyment of it, were real covenants, and bound the assignee. There was held to be in that case such a privity of estate between the parties as made the covenant run with the land.

In the case of the *Trustee of Watertown* v. *Cowen*, (4 Paige, 510,) it was held by Chancellor Walworth that a covenant by the grantor in a conveyance of lands in fee not to erect a building on a common or square owned by him, in front of the premises conveyed, was a covenant running with the land, and passed to a subsequent grantee of the premises without any special assignment of the covenant. Decisions embracing the same principle were made in *Hill* v. *Miller*, (3 Paige, 254,) and *Barrow* v. *Richard*, (8 id. 351,) In none of these cases was there any relation of tenure between the parties.

The ordinary cases of covenants of warranty, for quiet enjoyment and against incumbrances, in conveyances in fee, are familiar examples of covenants running with the land where no tenure exists.

The answer which is given to these cases by those who contend that the presence of tenure is necessary to enable covenants to run with the land, is that the *benefit* of covenants may run with the land without tenure, but that the *burden* cannot.

That distinction cannot be reconciled with the decisions in *Brewster* v. *Kidgell* and *Holmes* v. *Buckley*, *Moore* v. *Aldrich*, or *The Trustees of Watertown* v. *Cowen*, above cited ; and it has been repudiated in this court in the case of *Van Rensselaer* v. *Hays*, before referred to. Clearly therefore, the presence of tenure is not necessary to enable covenants, either as to their benefits or their burdens, to run with land.

If the relation of landlord and tenant between the parties were, as has been claimed, necessary to render covenants assignable, it would not be difficult to show that that relation exists in this case. A rent charge in fee with the right of entry for default in payment, although not constituting a reversion creates an *interest in the land* out of which the rent issues. (*Jemmot* v. *Cooley*, 1 Lev. 170, S. C.; 1 Saund. 112; 2 John. Cases, 26.)

The payments covenanted to be made in this case are not, as is claimed by the defendant's counsel, purchase money payments, but rent payments, although the conveyance of the land in fee constituted the consideration of the grant of the rent. The payments are as

56

clearly rent as they would have been it the like rent had been granted
for the same consideration by the original covenantor out of other
lands previously owned by him. (Littleton, §§ 217, 218, 219; Co.
Litt. 143 b. 144 a.)

In many of the cases in our courts between parties similarly situat-
ed, they have been spoken of and treated as landlords and tenants,
and the decisions in the cases of *Van Rensselaer rs. Snyder* (13 N. Y.,
299,) and *Van Rensselaer rs. Ball,* (19 id. 100,) can be sustained on
no o her ground, as they depended entirely up n a statute applicable
only to parties holding that relation (2 R. S., 505, § 30.) The other
branch of the objection is, that covenants can run only with land.
All the reasons t r holding covenants relating to lands assignable
appl. wi h equal force to covenants relating to incorporated hereditaments (Platt on covenants, 461, *Norman vs. Wells,* 17 Wen, 146.)
The direction of Lord Holt in *Brewster vs. Kidgell,* supra, is that the
covenant t r the payment of a rent charge in fee would run with the
rent, but the ca-e did not involve that question, as the action was by
the original cov nan ee. The opinion of Mr. Sugden, as has been
seen, concurs with that of Lord Holt, and it has been decided in England that a covenant runs with a lease of tithes, which, like rents,
are mere incorporeal hereditaments. (*Bally vs. Wells,* 3 Wils., 25,
30; 2. Smith's Leading Cases, 3 Law. Libr. Ed., 125; Note to Spencer's case). The case of *Holmes vs. Buckley,* and *Morse against Aldrich,* supra, where covenants were held to run with grants of a water
course, and of a right to dig and remove soil, are to the sume effect,
those grants not giving to the grantee any title to lands, but only
easements in the lands of the grantors. It is a settled proposition,
therefore, that covenants may run with incorporeal as well as with
corporeal hereditaments. But the question is not an open one in this
state, whether covenants for the payment of rents pass to the assignee
of the rents, without the aid of any reversion in the assignee. In the
case of *Demorest vs. Willard* (8 Cow., 206), the plaintiff had leased a
house and lot to the d ten ants for two years at an annual rent of
$600, payable quarter y. The defendant covenanted to pay the rent,
and to deliver up the premises at the end of the term in good repair.
The action was brought upon the covenant after the exp ration of the
term, the plaintiff claiming for rent in arrear, and damages because
the premises were not delivered up in good repair. It was shown
on the part of the defendants that the plaintiff had assigned the lease
to one Haswell, with all the rents to become due and payable during
the term. The court held that our statute to enable grantees of reversions to take advantage of conditions, to be performed by lessees,
had no application to the case, as the reversion had not been granted
to Haswell. But it wes nevertheless held, "that Haswell might sue
for and recover the rent in arrears, and consequently the plaintiff
could not." There had been a re-assignment of the arrears of rent
by Haswell, after the expiration of the term, to the plaintiff. In regard to that, Ch. J. Savage, who delivered the opinion of the court,
said: "The re-assignment by Haswell to the plaintiff was perfectly
useless in respect to the maintaining the suit. Arrears of rent are a
chose in action; and *not assignable like accruing rent.* Haswell was

assignee of the rent, and the whole became due before the reassign-
ment. *If the plaintiff can recover the arrears, it must be in the name of
Haswell.*

The Ch. Justice in his opinion also refers to a case between Little-
wood and Jackson, which had been decided by the same court seven
years earlier (in 1820), in which the plaintiff who was assignee of
1550 years of a term of 1590 years, having no interest in the reversion, was held entitled to recover for nine years rent, which fell due
during the portion of the term assigned to him. The Ch. J. said "as
I understand this case it decides that the assignee of the rent may recover it in that character without being assignee of the reversion."
The ruling in the cases has been repeatedly followed since, both by
the Supreme Court and the Court of Chancery (*Willard* v. *Tillman*,
19 Wend., 358; *Same* v. *Same*, 2 Hill, 274; *Childs* v. *Clark*, 3 Barb.,
52). In the case last cited the plaintiff, as the assignee of the
lease and rents for seven years out of a term of twenty years, filed a
bill against the assignees of the lessee, to recover arrears of rent
which became due to him during his portion of the term, the original
lessee being insolvent. On demurrer the chancellor dismissed the bill
on the ground that the plaintiff, as assignee of the rent, had a perfect
remedy at law, against the assignee of the lessee to recover such
rent. In his opinion the chancellor says, It is settled both in this state
and in England that an assignment *creates such a privity of estate* between the assignee and the lessee that the former may maintain a suit
in his own name for the rent which accrues and becomes payable
while such privity of estate exists." (see *Ards* v. *Watkins*, Cro. Eliz.,
637, 651; *Allen* v. *Bryan*, 5 B. and C., 512, *Stevenson* v. *Lombard*, 2
East., 576). In the case cited from 2 Hill, 274, Bronson, J., expressed some dissatisfaction with the previous cases, "but," he added "the
right of the assignee of the rent to sue in his own name was recognized by this court in *Demarest* v. *Willard*, and we ought not now depart
from that doctrine." The reasoning of the learned justice shows that
his doubts arose from the recognition of the doctrine that tenure, in
its feudal sense, was necessary to enable covenants to run with land
or real estate, a doctrine which, I think, the cases show can not be
sustained. These cases related to leases for years only, but the doctrine of maintenance which alone stands in the plaintiff's way is
equally applicable to temporary and to perpetual covenants, and if for
any reason temporary covenants should be excepted from its influence
there is much greater reason for excepting perpetual covenants of like
character. It appears to me, therefore, to be substantially settled
that there is such a privity of estate between the assignee of the rent
who from the fact that it is by law assignable, is entitled to demand
and receive it, and the assignee of the land out of which it issues,
and who is bound by the covenant of his assignee to pay it, that the
former without any reversion in the land can maintain an action, on
the covenant, at law, against the latter, and that there is no distinction in this respect between a rent in fee and one for life or years.
This conclusion renders it unnecessary to consider at much length
the question as to the effect of the code of procedure upon the rights
and liabilities of the parties under the covenant in question. Still, as

the only objection which existed, at common law, to the assignment of merely personal covenants so as to give a right of action to the assignee grew out of the doctrine of maintenance which has been entirely abolished in this state so far as relates to ordinary choses in action by the code of procedure, (§§ 111, 112), I do not see why the assignee of the rent could not now maintain an action on the covenant for the payment of such rent, in his own name, against any person bound by the covenant to pay it whether the benefit of the covenant did or did not run, at common law, with the rent, chapter 197 of the laws of 1805, would have had the same effect upon the present action if it had not been superceded by the more comprehensive provisions of the code, to which reference has been made.

The abolition of the doctrine of maintenance has no bearing upon the question of the liability of the assignee of the land to an action upon the covenants of his assignor, but that liability, at common law, was shown to exist in the case of Van Rensselaer v. Hays, supra, leaving undetermined only the question in whose name such liability could be enforced. If any doubt can be held to exist in regard to the liability of the defendant to the plaintiff in an action at law upon the covenant, there is none whatever as to his liability in equity, (19 N. Y., 85), and the merger, so far as relates to the forms of proceedings of legal and equitable remedies, by the code of procedure, would entitle the plaintiff to maintain the action on that ground, the case containing all the facts which are necessary to show his equitable right (Brewster v. Kidgell, 12 Mod., 166; The City of London v. Richmond, 2 Vern., 421; Keppel v. Bailey, 2 Myl. & Kee., 517; Tulk v. Moxhay, 2 Phil., 779; Livingston v. Livingston, 4 John., ch. 287; Rawle on Covenants, 298, 300).

In my opinion, however, the right of the plaintiff to recover in this case is entirely clear upon the ground that the covenants at common law, run, as was said by Mr. Sugden, with the rent, in the hands of the assignee so as to enable him to sue upon them; and with the land itself in the hands of the assignee so as to render him liable to be sued upon them; and that for that reason the judgment should be affirmed.

(Copy). E. PESHINE SMITH,
State Reporter.

In the Court of Appeals.

STEPHEN VAN RENSSELAER agt. ALBERT SLINGERLAND.

SELDEN, J. In the two cases of *Van Rensselaer v. Snyder*, 13 N. Y., 299, and *Van Rensselaer v. Ball*, (19 id., 100), all the objections which are urged against the recovery in this case, on facts, in all material respects, the same as those which are here presented, were considered and held insufficient to prevent a recovery. But in the case of *Van Rensselaer v. Ball*, the objections that the right of re-entry for condition broken was not assignable, and that no reversion remained in the plaintiff's devisor after his conveyance, and consequently the plaintiff

59

had no estate in the premises claimed, were answered by reference to
the statute (ch. 98 of 1805), by which all the provisions of the act of
1788, entitled "An act to enable grantees of reversions to take advantage of the conditions to be performed by lessees," and the remedies thereby given, were extended as well to grants or leases in fee
reserving rents, as to leases for life and years. Without the aid of
that act, it was assumed that the action could not be maintained, for
the reason that the provisions of the act of 1788 only extended to per·
sons entitled to reversions; and that, at common law, a right of entry
for condition broken, was not assignable. Since that decision was
pronounced, the act of 1805 has been repealed by the legislature, so
far as it applied to deeds of conveyance in fee, made prior to the 9th
day of April. 1805 (ch. 396 of 1860). The objection to the constitutionality of this act, as applied to cases like the present, has already
been overruled by this court; and as that act became a law prior to
the time of the trial of the present action, the rulings of the judge
can gain no support from the act of 1805. The absence of the pro·
visions of that act is, however, fully supplied, so far as those provisions relate to the questions under consideration in this case, by the
third section of chapter 274, of the Laws of 1846. The first section
of that act abolishes distress for rent. The second section repeals
several sections of the Revised Statutes, giving landlords, to a certain
extent, priority of claim for the payment of rent over the lien of exe-
cutions levied upon goods of tenants on demised premises. The third
section is as follows: " § 3. Whenever the right of re-entry is reserved
and given to a grantor or lessor in any grant or lease, in default of a
sufficiency of goods and chattels whereon to distrain for the satisfaction of any rent due, such re-entry may be made at any time after
default in the payment of such rent, provided fifteen days' previous
notice of such intention to re-enter, in writing, be given by such
grantor or lessor, or his heirs or assigns, to the grantee or lessee, his
heirs, executors. administrators or assigns, notwithstanding there
may be a sufficiency of goods and chattels on the lands granted or
demised for the satisfaction thereof. The said notice may be served
personally on such grantee or lessee, or by leaving it at his dwelling-
house on the premises."
This statute, in the cases to which it applies (and it is directly applicable to this case) accomplishes two objects: 1. It substitutes the
notice of fifteen days in the place of evidence that there was no sufficient distress on the demised or granted premises to pay the rent, and
makes such notice equivalent, in giving a right of re-entry to such
evidence, (*Van Rensselaer v. Snyder, supra*). 2. It recognizes the assignable quality of the condition of re-entry, and secures to the
assignee the same rights in that respect which were possessed by the
assignor to whom the right was originally reserved. The question,
therefore, is the same as it would be if the original grantor of the
premises, to whom the rent was reserved, were himself plaintiff in
this action. If he were the plaintiff, and depended upon the act of
1846 alone. although he would be excused (having given the fifteen
days' notice) from showing the want of sufficient distress upon the
premises. he would still be required to show a demand of the rent,

with all the technical precision which was required by the common law to effect a forfeiture of the tenant's estate. But the Revised Statutes have relieved the landlord from the necessity of making such demand where a half year's rent or more is in arrear, making the service of a declaration in ejectment to stand instead of such demand (2 R. S., 505, § 1); and this provision has been held applicable as well to grants in fee reserving rent as to leases for life or years. (*Van Rensselaer* v. *Snyder, supra*).

The plaintiff in this case proved all the facts which are required to be proved under these two statutes, to justify a recovery, or an action in the nature of ejectment, if ejectment is a proper remedy to gain possession of lands, wi hout previous entry, on breach of condition for re-entry on default in payment of rent. No entry is necessary to maintain the action, in any case where the immediate right of possession exists in the plaintiff (2 R. S., 303, § 3; 396. 307; 505, § 30; 4 Seld., 118). The statute introduced no new rule on this subject (Roscoe on Real actions, 497; 3 Co. Litt. Thomas, ed. 15, note 1). The cases of *Van Rensselaer* v. *Snyder* and *Van Rensselaer* v. *Ball*, are, in effect, decisive of the present action. The only distinction between them arises from the partial repeal of the act of 1805. Since those actions were tried, the place of which, so far as relates to the questions arising here, is perfectly supplied by the act of 1846, which still remains in force. The objections that the plaintiff has no reversion, and that a condition of re-entry can only operate by putting an end to an estate and can not give an estate to a stranger to the title, would have been no answer to the action, even at common law. It was decided by the unanimous opinion of the judges of the King's Bench in the case of *Jemot* v. *Cooley*, which was three times argued, that the grantee of a rent-charge in fee, without interest in the land beyond that given to him by such grant, could maintain ejectment after default in the payment of the rent. In the opinions, Kelyng, Twisden and Wyndham, justices, are reported to have said that "The power of entry is an inheritance and descends to the heir" (1 Lev., 170). The case is also reported in T. Ray, 135, 158; 1 Saund., 112; 1 Sid., 223, 261, 344. In that case the grantee of the rent-charge had entered and n ade a lease to the plaintiff in the ejectment; but, as 1 ' en shown above, entry was not necessary. The right of entry must exist before a lawful entry can be made, and that right is all which is required to maintain the action the only statutory aid which the plaintiff in the present case required, was that his right as assignee of the right of entry should be recognized, (2 Seld., 506, 507) which was done by the act of 1846.

The judgment should be affirmed. Wright, J., did not vote in this case, nor Rosekrans, J., who was absent; all the other judges concurred.

(Copy).

E. PESHINE SMITH,
State Reporter.

www.ingramcontent.com/pod-product-compliance
Lightning Source LLC
Chambersburg PA
CBHW021634270326
41931CB00008B/1025